Introvert's
DISNEYLAND TRAVEL
For Crowd Haters

How to Avoid Crowds While Traveling to Disneyland

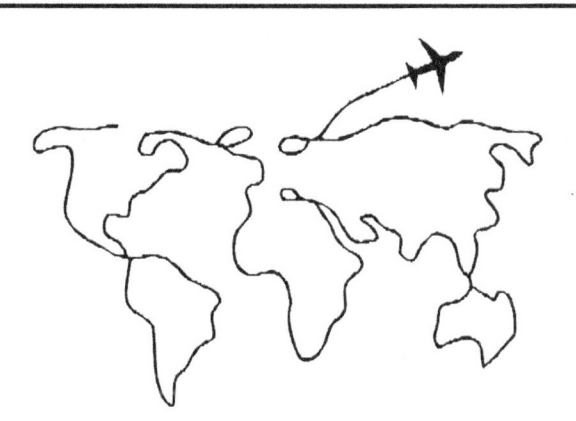

Linus Alden Knight

Contents

Introduction 1
Chapter 1: Understanding Disneyland's Crowd Patterns 6
    Overview of Peak Seasons and Their Impact on Crowd Levels 10
    Best Times to Visit: Off-Peak Days and Special Events 13
    How Weather Affects Crowd Sizes 17
Chapter 2: Planning Your Visit 22
    Section 1 25
    Choosing the Right Time.. 25
    Section 2 40
    Booking Strategies 40
Chapter 3: Hidden Gems in the Park 56
    Section 1 59
    Lesser-Known Attractions 59
    Section 2 73
    Serene Spots for Relaxation 73
Chapter 4: Navigating Popular Attractions 87
    Section 1 90
    Timing Your Visits 90
    Section 2 105
    Smart Approaches...105
Chapter 5: Enjoying Food and Drink Without the Rush 121
    Section 1 123
    Dining Options..123
    Section 2 136
    Relaxing Locations for Meals 136
Chapter 6: Embracing the Disneyland Experience 148

Section 1 151
Finding Your Own Pace 151
Section 2 163
Mindful Travel Practices 163
Conclusion 177

Introvert's Disneyland Travel for Crowd Haters   by Linus Alden Knight

Introduction

"The most delightful discoveries happen when the world thins out."

In the undulating sea of faces and the cacophony that defines the typical Disneyland experience, there exists a whisper of a promise: that even in such a crowd, one can find a pocket of calm—a personal Neverland. This is the heart and soul of **Introvert's Disneyland Travel for Crowd Haters**, a guide crafted not just from maps and schedules but from the quiet moments and soft havens found amidst the clamor of America's favorite theme park.

Picture the early morning mist clinging to the outlines of Sleeping Beauty's Castle, the hushed serenity of a walkway not yet caught in the day's tourist tide, or the golden light spilling

Introvert's Disneyland Travel for Crowd Haters   by Linus Alden Knight

silently across the park as the crowd's roar dims with the setting sun. These are the times and places within Disneyland where the introverted traveler thrives—where the magic of solitude wraps around the wonders of a place designed for the masses.

With its promise of fairy tales, Disneyland comes to life and realizes childhood dreams, beckoning millions to its gates each year. Yet, for the introverted traveler, such crowds can diminish the allure of this magical place, turning what should be a delightful adventure into a trial of endurance.

Through this book, I invite you to rediscover Disneyland, not through the pressing crowds and rushed visits, but through pathways less traveled and moments carefully curated. For those who feel their energy sap at the thought of jostling elbows for a view of the parade or those who seek to admire the intricate details of the park's design without the interruption of an impatient crowd, this is your guide. It's a tribute to the joys of traveling alone or in quiet companionship, of finding delight in the attractions and observing, unhurried and unencumbered.

Join me on a trip tailored for comfort, personal space, and the reclamation of wonder amid a lively world. Let's explore Disneyland as travelers and as quiet observers of a magical play, each scene ready to reveal its secrets to those who wait patiently in the wings.

Purpose of the Book

At the core of **Introvert's Disneyland Travel for Crowd Haters** is a singular, vital mission: to enable the introverted soul to navigate the exuberant chaos of Disneyland while preserving their inner peace and solitude. It is a blueprint and a manifesto, a detailed directory of strategies and an affirmation of the introverted traveler's need for space and quietude. Disneyland might be an emblem of communal joy and shared excitement, but it also harbors quiet corners and overlooked pathways where the magic burns just as brightly, albeit more softly.

The Magic of Disneyland Beyond the Crowds

Beyond the vibrant queues and the busy eateries, beyond the whirlwind of shows and parades, Disneyland harbors a different kind of magic—one that doesn't require you to elbow your way through crowds or strain your voice over the din. It's the magic of early morning dew still fresh on the Fantasyland flowers, the serene glow of lanterns in New Orleans Square as dusk falls, or the gentle lapping of the Rivers of America under a starlit sky. This section of the book delves deep into these less-trodden paths, offering a vision of Disneyland that goes beyond the typical fanfare to highlight its quieter, more reflective beauties.

This magic is subtle; it doesn't shout for your attention but waits patiently to be noticed. It's in the architectural marvels and the detailed craftsmanship of each themed land, in the stories embedded in each ride, waiting to be read by those who look closely enough. For the introvert, the joy of Disneyland can be found in these details—the artistic nuances that are often overshadowed by the park's more flamboyant attractions.

For instance, consider the delicate beauty of the Japanese tea garden in Adventureland, a spot many pass but few truly see. Or the historical exhibits and art displays in the lobby of the Great Moments with Mr. Lincoln theater, where the echoes of past guests are just whispers, allowing you a moment of connection with the narratives held within the walls.

Exploring Disneyland beyond the crowds means having the time and space to appreciate these elements. It means walking through Sleeping Beauty's Castle not just as a passageway to another land but as an enchanting experience unto itself, appreciating the intricate mosaics that recount Aurora's tale. It's about enjoying the street performances in Main Street, U.S.A., where the music swells just for you as if you're the guest of honor in this vast, lively home.

Overview of the Book Structure

The structure of this book is designed to ease your tour, starting with a comprehensive overview of how to plan your visit—from choosing the best times to what to bring to enhance your solitary experience. Following the introductory planning advice, the book is divided into chapters corresponding to different Disneyland and California Adventure Park areas. Each chapter offers insights into the best times to explore different attractions, tips for finding quiet spots even during chaos, and how to use Disneyland's systems to your advantage as an introvert. Finally, the guide wraps up with a section on extending the tranquility beyond the park gates, suggesting nearby day trips and quieter alternatives that complement the Disney experience.

This book is more than a guide; it is an invitation to explore Disneyland in a way that honors who you are. It promises that even in a place as lively and crowded as Disneyland, there are myriad ways to find joy and wonder in solitude and quiet. As you turn these pages, you will learn how to navigate the crowds and find your own path through the happiest place on Earth, making it a truly personal voyage marked by introspection and awe.

1 Chapter

Understanding Disneyland's Crowd Patterns

Exploring Disneyland often feels like exploring a vibrant city: its rhythms and flows are dictated by the patterns of its visitors. For the introverted traveler, understanding these patterns is beneficial and essential for a serene tour through this animated world. Let's discover the predictable rhythms of Disneyland, providing you with a roadmap to anticipate the ebbs and flows of its crowds. Armed with this knowledge, you can plan your visit to coincide with quieter periods, ensuring a more personal and less pressured visit.

The Pulse of the Park

Disneyland's crowd patterns can often be predicted accurately that borders on the uncanny. Seasonal events, school holidays, and even the time of day can transform the park from a quiet wonderland into a teeming mass of excited tourists. The first step to mastering your visit is understanding these shifts.

- **Seasonal Swings:** Disneyland's busiest periods typically align with summer, Christmas, and spring break school vacations. However, there are magical windows—often in mid-January or late February—when the crowds thin significantly. These off-peak times are ideal for those who prefer minimal human interaction and maximum enjoyment of the park's offerings.

- **Weekly Waves:** Weekends naturally attract larger crowds, with locals and tourists descending on the park. In contrast, mid-week visits, particularly on Tuesdays and Wednesdays, usually see lower attendance. These days can offer a more relaxed pace, allowing you to explore at your leisure without the hustle of larger crowds.

- **Daily Dynamics:** The time of day significantly affects crowd density. Mornings are often quieter as the gates open and the world of Disney just begins to stir. Many guests do not arrive until later, making early morning hours a golden time for introverts to enjoy popular attractions with shorter wait times. Conversely, evenings see a resurgence of visitors, especially before the night shows and parades.

Using Technology to Track Crowds

Nowadays, various tools and apps are at your disposal to help track real-time crowd levels at Disneyland. These resources can be invaluable for planning your visit, offering insights into which park areas are busiest at any given time, and predicting wait times for rides.

- **Mobile Apps:** Apps like Disneyland's official app provide real-time updates on ride wait times and park capacity levels. These can be used to adjust your itinerary on the fly, steer clear of overcrowded areas, and optimize your visit.

- **Crowd Calendars:** Several websites offer crowd calendars based on historical data and current trends. These calendars predict crowd levels for each day of the year, advising you on the best times to visit. Utilizing this data can help you choose a day for your trip when the park is least likely to be crowded.

Strategies for Avoiding Crowds

With a good understanding of when Disneyland is busiest, you can craft strategies to navigate the park in ways that keep you comfortably distant from the densest throngs of visitors.

- **Early Access and Late Stays:** Arriving early allows you to enjoy popular attractions with shorter queues and gives you the pleasure of experiencing the park's opening ceremony—a magical start to any day. Similarly, staying late can be advantageous. As many families with young children leave after the fireworks, the park offers a quieter atmosphere.

- **Ride Reservation Systems:** Disneyland's FastPass and MaxPass systems allow you to reserve access to certain attractions, reducing the time you spend in line. By planning these reservations around typical crowd peaks, you can ensure a smoother, less crowded experience.

- **Alternative Attractions:** While big-name rides draw the largest crowds, Disneyland is filled with lesser-known attractions that often go unnoticed. These can offer shorter wait times and a more relaxed atmosphere away from the busy main paths.

Overview of Peak Seasons and Their Impact on Crowd Levels

Here's an overview of the intricacies of Disneyland's peak seasons, providing insights into how various times of the year affect visitor density and how you can leverage this knowledge to enjoy a more secluded visit.

- **Summer Vacation (June through August):** As one of the quintessential family destinations, Disneyland sees a significant surge in attendance during the summer months. Families take advantage of school breaks to visit, leading to some of the year's highest crowd levels. The warm weather and extended park hours offer more time to explore and enjoy the attractions, but they also mean more people to navigate around. Planning your visit early in the morning or later in the evening during these months can help mitigate the impact of the crowds.

- **Winter Holidays (Mid-December through Early January):** The winter holiday season is another peak period at Disneyland, with the park decked out in festive decorations and special holiday-themed events and parades. This season draws large crowds eager to experience the holiday magic, resulting in longer wait times and heavily populated areas. However, the breathtaking holiday decor and unique seasonal attractions make it a tempting time despite the crowds. Visiting on weekdays or the first few hours after opening can provide a slightly less crowded experience.

- **Spring Break (March through Mid-April):** Spring break brings another influx of visitors, with families, college students, and young adults flocking to the park. This season is particularly popular due to the pleasant weather and the bloom of spring, making the park exceptionally picturesque. The crowd levels vary, with some days seeing peak holiday numbers. Utilizing crowd calendars and planning visits on less popular days can help you avoid the worst of the spring break rush.

- **Halloween Season (September through October):** Disneyland's Halloween celebrations are a growing draw. The park transforms with spooky decorations, special merchandise, and themed attractions like the Haunted Mansion Holiday makeover. While not as crowded as the summer or winter holidays, weekends during the Halloween season can still see significant visitor numbers. Weekdays, especially earlier in the week, are less crowded and ideal for those looking to experience the festive atmosphere without the dense crowds.

- **Thanksgiving Week:** As a family-oriented holiday, Thanksgiving week sees a notable increase in park attendance. Families use the holiday break as an opportunity for a vacation, and Disneyland's Thanksgiving and Christmas decorations are fully on display, adding to the allure. The week leading up to Thanksgiving and the weekend following are particularly busy.

Strategies to Mitigate Crowd Impact: To make the most of your Disneyland visit during these peak times, consider the following strategies:

- **Advance Planning:** Purchase tickets and make reservations well in advance. Utilize Disneyland's reservation system to book access to popular attractions, reducing time spent in lines.

- **Utilize FastPass and MaxPass:** These systems allow you to skip long lines for popular rides. Planning your FastPass selections around peak times can help you avoid the largest crowds.

- **Early Entry and Late Stays:** Take advantage of early entry days if you stay at a Disneyland resort hotel. Also, staying in the park late can allow you to enjoy popular attractions with significantly shorter wait times, as many guests leave after the fireworks.

- **Mid-Week Visits:** Plan your visit for mid-week. Tuesdays and Wednesdays are typically the least crowded days at Disneyland, providing a more relaxed atmosphere.

- **Off-Season Exploration:** If your schedule allows, visiting during the off-season (late January through early March, late April through early June) can result in a more enjoyable experience with fewer people and shorter lines.

- **Stay Informed:** Watch real-time crowd-tracking apps and websites during your visit. Flexibility and willingness to adjust your plan based on current crowd levels can make your day much more enjoyable.

Best Times to Visit: Off-Peak Days and Special Events

For introverts and those who prefer a more relaxed visit, choosing the right time to explore Disneyland is as crucial as deciding what attractions to see. This section delves into the optimal times for visiting—focusing on off-peak periods and highlighting special events that offer unique experiences without the overwhelming crowds.

Off-Peak Days: A Quieter Disneyland Experience

- **Late Winter and Early Spring (Late January to Early March):** After the holiday decorations come down and before spring break crowds begin, Disneyland experiences one of its quietest periods. The cooler weather and chance of rain reduce attendance, making this an ideal time for introverts to enjoy the parks. The lines are shorter, and taking in the sights and sounds is easier without the hustle and bustle.

- **Late Spring (After Spring Break to Just Before Memorial Day):** Late April and May can provide a sweet spot for visiting Disneyland. Most schools are still in session, and the summer tourist season has not started. This period allows for enjoying the mild weather and the full range of attractions without summer's intense crowds.

- **Early Fall (After Labor Day to Mid-October):** Once children return to school in September, the crowd levels drop significantly. This time also coincides with the beginning of the Halloween season at Disneyland, offering themed decorations and special events in a less crowded environment.

- **Mid-November (After Veterans Day to Just Before Thanksgiving Week):** This brief window between holidays is another excellent time for those looking to avoid large crowds. Additionally, visitors can experience the magic of the park's Christmas decorations starting to go up, providing a festive atmosphere without the peak holiday crowds.

Special Events: Unique Times to Experience Magic

Disneyland hosts several special events throughout the year that cater to different interests and can enhance your visit. These events often occur during times that might otherwise be considered off-peak, adding value to visiting during quieter periods.

- **Disneyland After Dark:** These specially ticketed evening events allow a limited number of guests into the park after hours. Themes vary from sweethearts' night to 80s night, offering unique entertainment, specialty foods, and the chance to enjoy the rides with minimal waits. For introverts, these events can provide a comfortable way to experience the park's excitement with more space to breathe.
- **Food & Wine Festival:** Held in the spring at California Adventure, this festival combines Californian cuisine and

beverages with the fun of Disney. It's less crowded than other times, especially if attended on a weekday, and offers a more adult-oriented atmosphere that can be particularly appealing to introverts looking for a different type of Disney experience.

- **Halloween Time:** While Halloween at Disneyland can draw crowds, especially during Mickey's Halloween Party, September and October also offer quieter days. The park is transformed with unique Halloween-themed decor and special attractions like the Haunted Mansion Holiday overlay.

- **Festival of Holidays:** Running from November through early January at California Adventure, this event celebrates diverse cultural festivities with music, dance, and food. Visiting on weekdays in late November or early December can allow you to enjoy the festival's offerings before the Christmas crowd surge.

Tips for Planning Your Visit During Special Events and Off-Peak Days

- **Book Early:** Special events and off-peak times can be popular among those in the know, so planning and booking your trip well in advance is wise.

- **Stay Nearby:** Choosing accommodation close to the parks can allow you to return to your hotel for a break during the day, making your visit more enjoyable and less exhausting.

- **Arrive Early or Stay Late:** Regardless of when you visit, arriving early or staying late can help you experience popular attractions with shorter wait times.

- **Check Park Hours:** Park hours can vary greatly depending on the season and day of the week. Checking the hours can help you maximize your time in the parks.

- **Arrive Early or Stay Late:** Regardless of when you visit, getting to the park early or staying late can help you avoid the largest crowds. Many guests do not arrive first thing in the morning and tend to leave after the evening entertainment.

- **Utilize Technology:** Use apps and websites that provide real-time updates on crowd levels and attraction wait times. This technology can help you navigate the park more efficiently during your visit.

How Weather Affects Crowd Sizes

Weather plays a significant role in shaping the crowd sizes at Disneyland, often acting as a natural moderator of visitor flow. Understanding the impact of different weather conditions can help you strategically choose the best days for your visit, particularly if you prefer a quieter experience. This section

Introvert's Disneyland Travel for Crowd Haters		by Linus Alden Knight

explores how various weather scenarios can influence crowd behavior and provides tips on using this knowledge to your advantage.

Impact of Weather on Disneyland Crowds

- **Sunny and Warm Days:** Traditionally, sunny and warm days attract the largest crowds to Disneyland. The pleasant weather is ideal for exploring the park and enjoying outdoor attractions and shows. These are the days when the iconic image of a crowded Disneyland comes to life, with families and tourists filling the walkways. If you prefer to avoid large crowds, choose a different day, particularly outside of peak tourist seasons.

- **Rainy Days:** Rain tends to deter many visitors, especially those with young children, which can lead to a significant drop in crowd sizes. While a rainy day might seem less than ideal for a theme park visit, it can provide a unique opportunity for those who don't mind a bit of wet weather. Lines for indoor attractions are shorter, and the overall ambiance of the park can feel more relaxed and quiet—a rare occurrence in such a usually vibrant place.

- **Cooler Temperatures:** As the temperature drops, particularly during the off-peak seasons of late fall and winter, so do the crowd levels. Cooler weather makes for a more comfortable experience away from the often oppressive heat of summer. These days are perfect for enjoying the park leisurely, taking time to appreciate the thematic details and immersive environments without the pressure of long lines and waiting times.

- **Extreme Weather Conditions:** On occasions when the weather turns extreme, such as during a heatwave or a severe storm, Disneyland may see a drastic reduction in visitors. While extreme heat may slow down your pace, strategic planning—such as focusing on indoor, air-conditioned attractions—can make the visit more bearable and surprisingly crowd-free.

Strategies for Weather-Wise Visiting

- **Check the Weather Forecast:** Before planning your trip, check the weather forecast. Look for days that might be slightly off-peak regarding weather desirability. For example, a forecast of light, intermittent rain might deter casual visitors but still offer you several hours of comfortable park time.

- **Dress Appropriately:** If you choose to visit on a day with less-than-ideal weather, dress appropriately. Comfortable, water-resistant clothing and shoes for rainy days or light, breathable fabrics for hot days can make your experience much more enjoyable.

- **Take Advantage of Indoor Attractions:** On rainy or extremely hot days, focus your visit on indoor attractions. Disneyland offers numerous indoor rides, shows, and experiences that can provide entertainment away from the harsh elements.

- **Visit During Unpredictable Weather:** If you're flexible, consider visiting on days when the weather might be unpredictable. Many potential visitors will avoid booking their trips on such days, leading to smaller crowds and shorter lines.

- **Utilize Early Morning and Late Evening Hours:** Weather can often be more extreme in the middle of the day. Planning your activities during the early morning or late evening can help you avoid the discomfort of midday sun, rain, or cold.

- **Stay Hydrated and Prepared:** Whatever the weather, staying hydrated is crucial. On hot days, bring a refillable water bottle. A warm beverage can keep your spirits on cooler or rainy days. Always carry essentials like sunscreen or a compact umbrella to enhance your comfort and readiness for any weather.

You can significantly enhance your Disneyland visit by considering the weather's impact on crowd sizes and behavior. Whether braving a rainy day for shorter lines or enjoying the calm of a cool winter, the weather can be a powerful ally in crafting a more personal and enjoyable theme park experience.

Chapter 2

Planning Your Visit

Starting a trip to Disneyland requires more than just a ticket; it demands a strategy, especially for those who prefer to sidestep the heavy crowds and soak in the park's magic at a more contemplative pace.

Planning a trip to Disneyland is akin to preparing for a trip to a small, vibrant city whose pathways are lined with adventures and surprises at every turn. However, the excitement of this tour can often be overshadowed by the prospect of navigating through overwhelming crowds and managing logistical challenges. For introverts and those who revel in peaceful exploration, the key to a fulfilling visit lies in thoughtful preparation and strategic timing.

Understanding the Layout

Begin by familiarizing yourself with the layout of Disneyland. The park is divided into several thematic lands, offering unique attractions, dining options, and entertainment. Understanding these lands' geography and relative proximity can help you optimize your route, minimizing unnecessary backtracking and conserving energy for enjoying the attractions.

Selecting the Right Date

Choosing the right date is crucial. Consider visiting during off-peak seasons when the crowds are thinner. Mid-week days (Tuesday through Thursday) generally have lower attendance rates than weekends. Also, watch the park's calendar for special events or planned refurbishments that might affect crowd levels or close down certain attractions.

Purchasing Tickets and Reservations

Advance ticket purchases are a must. Disneyland now requires all visitors to make a reservation for the day of their visit, which can be done when purchasing your ticket online. This system helps manage the park's capacity and ensures a better experience for all guests. Consider also purchasing tickets to special experiences or dining reservations that can enhance your visit, such as character dining or guided tours that align with your interests.

FastPass and MaxPass

Leveraging Disneyland's FastPass system is a smart move. This service allows you to reserve access to select attractions and skip the regular lines. For an even more streamlined experience, you might opt for Disney's MaxPass, which allows you to make FastPass selections directly from your smartphone and includes digital downloads of any photos captured by Disneyland photographers during your visit.

Planning Your Day

Once the logistics are handled, plan your day with precision. Start early by arriving before the park opens to take advantage of shorter lines in the first few hours of the day. Prioritize attractions on your must-see list and use the Disneyland app to monitor wait times throughout the day to adjust your plan as needed.

Dining and Breaks

Decide in advance where you would like to eat. Disneyland offers many dining options, from quick-service snacks to upscale restaurants. Reservations are recommended for sit-down restaurants, especially during peak times. Don't forget to schedule breaks throughout your day to rest and recharge. Find quieter areas in the park to relax, or schedule a sit-down meal during the busiest hours of the afternoon when you'll appreciate a break from the crowds the most.

Special Needs and Accommodations

If you or anyone in your travel party has special needs, Disneyland is equipped to accommodate. Contact guest services to discuss any necessary arrangements, from disability access to dietary restrictions, to ensure your visit is comfortable and enjoyable.

Section 1

Choosing the Right Time

Selecting the optimal time to visit Disneyland is crucial for anyone looking to experience the park's enchantment minus the usual crowds. This decision can make or break the enjoyment of the entire trip for introverts and those who savor quieter atmospheres.

What are Peak and Off-Peak Seasons?

The first step in planning your visit is understanding the distinction between peak and off-peak seasons. Peak seasons at Disneyland typically include summer months (June through August), major holidays like Christmas, New Year, Thanksgiving, and other special events such as Halloween and spring break periods. These times attract the largest crowds due to school vacations and holiday celebrations.

Conversely, off-peak periods—often found in late winter (January and February, excluding holiday weekends) and early spring (late April and early May)—see significantly fewer visitors. The weeks after Labor Day until just before Halloween in September and October also tend to be less crowded, excluding weekends and Halloween.

Weekday vs. Weekend Visits

The day of the week you choose to visit can also greatly impact crowd levels. Weekdays, particularly Tuesday through Thursday, generally experience lower attendance compared to weekends. Many local visitors and annual pass holders often visit on weekends, so planning a weekday trip can help avoid larger groups and longer lines.

Weather Considerations

Weather is another crucial factor when deciding on the best time to visit. Southern California is known for its mild climate, but temperatures can vary. The cooler months might deter some visitors but can provide a more comfortable experience for those who prefer to avoid the heat. Although less common, rainy days usually result in the lowest crowd levels and can be an ideal time for visitors who don't mind donning a raincoat.

Special Events and Limited-Time Offerings

Disneyland hosts several special events and promotions throughout the year, which can significantly affect crowd sizes. Events like the Food & Wine Festival, Star Wars Celebration, or Disney's anniversary celebrations can draw larger crowds. However, these events also offer unique experiences that aren't available at other times, providing special parades, shows, and themed attractions that might be worth braving the crowds for some.

Early Park Hours and Late Nights

Another strategy to consider is taking advantage of early park hours and late nights. Disneyland occasionally offers resort guests Magic Hours or similar benefits, allowing early entry to the park before it opens to the public. These times can provide a serene atmosphere as the crowds are much smaller. Likewise, staying late, especially during extended summer hours, allows you to enjoy cooler temperatures and lighter crowds, as many guests with young children tend to leave after the fireworks show.

Detailed Month-by-Month Guide to Visiting Disneyland

When planning your visit to Disneyland, considering the time of year can greatly affect the quality of your experience. Each month carries its own set of advantages and drawbacks, influenced by weather, crowd sizes, and special events. This detailed guide provides insights into what to expect each month at Disneyland, helping you choose the best time for a visit tailored to your preferences.

January

- **Crowds:** After the holiday season, crowd levels drop significantly, making January one of the best times to visit for those looking to avoid long lines.

- **Weather:** The weather is cooler, which is comfortable for walking around, though evenings can be chilly.

- **Considerations:** Some attractions may be closed for maintenance after the busy holiday season.

February

- **Crowds:** Like January, February is a low-crowd month, except during the Presidents' Day weekend.

- **Weather:** The weather remains cool, with occasional rain; check the forecast and prepare for intermittent showers.

- **Considerations:** Fewer hours of daylight mean less time to explore the park, though you can still cover a lot with reduced crowd levels.

March

- **Crowds:** Crowd sizes begin to increase towards the end of the month due to spring break.

- **Weather:** The weather starts warming up, making wandering the parks more pleasant.

- **Considerations:** The beginning of the month is quieter, so plan early March visits for a more peaceful experience.

April

- **Crowds:** Early April sees spring break crowds, but they taper off as the month progresses.

- **Weather:** Generally mild, perfect for spending all day outdoors.

- **Considerations:** Look out for special spring events, which can draw additional visitors.

May

- **Crowds:** Moderate, but start to pick up towards the end of the month leading into Memorial Day weekend.
- **Weather:** Warm and pleasant, ideal for enjoying all park areas.
- **Considerations:** This is a great time to catch the tail end of any spring festivities before the summer crowds arrive.

June

- **Crowds:** June begins the high season as schools let out for summer.
- **Weather:** Warm to hot; be prepared with sun protection and hydration.
- **Considerations:** Longer park hours begin, giving you more time to explore despite the crowds.

July

- **Crowds:** One of the busiest months due to summer vacation.
- **Weather:** Hot and busy; plan for midday breaks to avoid the heat.

- **Considerations:** Enjoy the full swing of summer programming, including nightly fireworks and special shows.

August

- **Crowds:** Still busy, especially early in the month, but start to lessen towards the end.
- **Weather:** Similar to July, hot and sunny.
- **Considerations:** Take advantage of late summer visits for slightly reduced crowd levels and enjoy extended hours and summer events.

September

- **Crowds:** After Labor Day, crowds decrease significantly.
- **Weather:** On warm days with cooler evenings, the weather turns pleasant.
- **Considerations:** Halloween decorations and themed events begin, drawing fans of Disney's Halloween celebrations.

October

- **Crowds:** Moderate, but Halloween events can attract more visitors, especially during weekends.
- **Weather**: Mild; perfect for costumes if you attend any Halloween parties.

- **Considerations:** Don't miss the Halloween festivities, among the most popular seasonal events.

November

- **Crowds:** Early November is quiet, but Thanksgiving week shows a significant attendance spike.

- **Weather:** Cooler, with an increased chance of rain; layering is key.

- **Considerations:** The holiday season starts mid-month, with festive decorations and themed events adding to the magic.

December

- **Crowds:** Early December is manageable, but crowds peak closer to Christmas and New Year's Eve.

- **Weather:** Cool. It is often the coldest month of the year at Disneyland, though it is still milder than many other places.

- **Considerations:** Experience the full festive season with holiday parades, seasonal treats, and perhaps the most magical time to see Disneyland.

Choosing the right month for your Disneyland visit depends on what you value most: lower crowds, special events, or ideal weather. By planning with these factors in mind, you can optimize your experience to enjoy the magic of Disneyland with the least amount of stress and the most enjoyment.

Identifying Less Crowded Days of the Week

A trip to Disneyland can vary significantly depending on the day of the week you choose to visit. While weekends typically see a surge in attendance, weekdays offer a different, often more subdued atmosphere, allowing for a more relaxed and enjoyable experience. This section will guide you through identifying the best days to visit Disneyland to avoid large crowds, making your adventure magical and serene.

Daily Crowd Patterns

Several factors, including local school schedules, holidays, and typical tourist behavior, influence crowd size dynamics throughout the week. Here's a detailed look at what to expect from each day:

Monday

- **Crowd Levels:** Moderate. Mondays can still be busy, particularly as tourists extend their weekend trips. However, they are generally less crowded than on weekends.

- **Strategy:** Use Monday as a transitional day to enjoy popular attractions that were too crowded over the weekend.

Tuesday

- **Crowd Levels:** Low. It is one of the least crowded days at Disneyland, making it ideal for visitors who prefer a quiet environment.

- **Strategy:** Take advantage of shorter lines to visit the most popular rides and attractions. It's also a great day to enjoy shows and parades with better viewing spots.

Wednesday

- **Crowd Levels:** Low. Like Tuesday, Wednesday sees reduced visitor numbers as it falls in the middle of the working week.

- **Strategy:** Continue exploring major attractions and perhaps revisit your favorites from Tuesday. Midweek is perfect for leisurely exploring smaller attractions and shops.

Thursday

- **Crowd Levels:** Moderate. Crowds begin to pick up slightly on Thursday as visitors arrive for an extended weekend.

- **Strategy:** If you started your visit on Tuesday or Wednesday, use Thursday to explore areas of the park you may have missed or those generally less crowded.

Friday

- **Crowd Levels:** High. As the weekend nears, Friday sees an influx of both local visitors and tourists starting their weekend getaways.

- **Strategy:** Fridays are best for experiencing the ambiance of a busier park or catching entertainment options that might be scaled down during the week.

Saturday and Sunday

- **Crowd Levels:** Very High. The weekend is the busiest time at Disneyland as families, locals, and tourists flock to the park.

- **Strategy**: If you must visit on a weekend, arrive early and prioritize must-see attractions first. Consider dining reservations to avoid long restaurant waits and use the Disneyland app to monitor and adjust to live crowd conditions.

Seasonal and Holiday Considerations

It's also important to consider the time of year when planning your visit. Holidays and school breaks can lead to atypical crowd patterns. For instance, weekdays during summer break or other school holidays can be just as crowded as weekends. Similarly, holiday weeks like Thanksgiving or Christmas can see peak attendance daily, with little variation in crowd levels from Monday to Sunday.

Leveraging Technology for Real-Time Decisions

To effectively navigate Disneyland on less crowded days, leverage technology:

- **Mobile Apps**: Disneyland's official app is invaluable for real-time crowd tracking, wait times, and finding the shortest lines for food and restrooms.

- **Crowd Calendars:** Online crowd calendars can provide historical data on attendance levels, helping you choose the best days to visit.

Benefits of Visiting on Less Crowded Days

Choosing to visit Disneyland on a less crowded day has numerous benefits:

- **Enhanced Experience:** Less time spent in lines means more time enjoying attractions, shows, and the overall ambiance of the park.

- **Interaction Quality:** With fewer guests, interactions with Disney characters and staff can be more personal and less rushed.

- **Spontaneity:** A less crowded park offers more flexibility to change plans spontaneously without the stress of navigating through dense crowds.

Special Events to Avoid or Embrace

Disneyland is renowned not just for its attractions but also for its calendar, which is packed with special events and celebrations. These occasions can dramatically affect crowd sizes and the overall park atmosphere, offering unique experiences that are either a must-see or a must-avoid, depending on your preferences.

Events to Embrace

- **Disneyland After Dark:** Held on select nights throughout the year, Disneyland After Dark is a series of separately ticketed evening events that feature unique themes like 80s Nite, Sweethearts' Nite, or Star Wars Nite. These events often include special entertainment, rare character greetings, and themed menu items. Crowds are more controlled due to limited ticket sales, making it an ideal event for those looking for a different Disneyland experience with manageable crowd levels.

- **Food & Wine Festival:** Occurring annually at Disney California Adventure, the Food & Wine Festival offers culinary delights from around the globe, cooking demonstrations, and live entertainment. While popular, the festival's spread-out nature across the park prevents the feeling of overcrowding. This event is perfect for food lovers looking to enjoy gourmet offerings in a festive yet relaxed atmosphere.

- **Run Disney Events:** The Run Disney races are a fun way to experience the parks in a non-traditional way. These events typically occur before the park opens to the general public and include races through both Disneyland and Disney California Adventure. Participating in or cheering on runners can provide an energizing start to the day, with reduced crowds and a unique park perspective.

- **Festival of Holidays:** Celebrating cultural diversity and holiday traditions, the Festival of Holidays features specialty food, music, and entertainment that reflect various cultural festivities. Held during the holiday season at Disney California Adventure, this event provides a celebratory experience without the overwhelming crowds found in Disneyland during the same time.

Events to Avoid

- **Halloween Time and Mickey's Halloween Party**: Halloween at Disneyland is incredibly popular, with extensive decorations, themed attractions, and Mickey's Halloween Party—a special ticketed event on select nights in September and October. These events attract large crowds, especially on party nights, which can significantly impact the overall experience with long lines and extended wait times.

- **Holiday Season (Mid-November through Early January):** The weeks from Thanksgiving through New Year's are among the busiest at Disneyland. The park is transformed with holiday decorations, special parades, and shows like the "Believe... In Holiday Magic" fireworks display. While magical, these weeks see some of the highest crowd levels of the year, which might be overwhelming for those seeking a quieter visit.

- **24-Hour Events and Major Anniversaries:** On rare occasions, Disneyland hosts 24-hour events or celebrates major anniversaries, drawing massive crowds of both locals and international visitors. These events, while festive and unique, often lead to unprecedented overcrowding and are generally best avoided by those who prefer a more laid-back Disneyland experience.

Strategies for Attending Special Events

- **Purchase Tickets Early**: For events that require a separate ticket, purchase yours as soon as they go on sale to ensure availability and typically lower prices.

- **Plan Your Visit**: If attending a special event, plan your visit around the event schedule. Arrive early or stay late to enjoy the park attractions when crowds are lighter.

- **Use Technology**: Leverage apps and websites to monitor crowd levels and wait times during events to optimize your visit.

Choosing which special events at Disneyland to attend can enhance your park experience, offering unique entertainment and celebrations not available at other times.

Section 2

Booking Strategies

Properly planning and booking your Disneyland trip can drastically enhance your experience, allowing you to enjoy the magic of the park with minimal hassle.

Advance Ticket Purchases and Reservations

- **Book Tickets Early:** Disneyland requires all visitors to have both a valid ticket and a park reservation for the same day. Given this, it's crucial to purchase your tickets and make your reservations as far in advance as possible, especially if you're visiting during peak times or want to attend special events. Buying tickets early ensures your entry and can also help in securing a better price, as ticket costs can fluctuate.

- **Understand Ticket Types:** Disneyland offers a variety of ticket types, including single-day, multi-day, park hopper options, and more. Evaluate your travel plans and decide which ticket best suits your itinerary. Multi-day tickets often offer better value and flexibility, particularly if you wish to experience everything without a rush.

Dining Reservations

- **Plan Ahead for Dining:** Popular restaurants in Disneyland, like the Blue Bayou or Oga's Cantina, can book up quickly, especially during peak seasons. Make dining reservations up to 60 days in advance to secure a spot at your preferred times and locations. This is particularly important if you are celebrating a special occasion or have dietary restrictions.

- **Mobile Ordering:** Take advantage of Disneyland's mobile ordering service through their app for quicker and more convenient dining at many quick-service restaurants. This can save you a significant amount of time, bypassing long lines during meal times.

Accommodations

- **Stay On-Site or Nearby:** Choosing where to stay can greatly influence your trip. Staying at one of Disneyland's resort hotels offers benefits like proximity to the parks, extra magic hours, and the ability to go back to your room easily for breaks during the day. However, nearby hotels might offer more budget-friendly options and still provide great convenience, especially if they offer shuttle services to the park gates.

- **Consider Travel Packages:** Sometimes, travel packages can provide good deals that include hotel stays, park tickets, and sometimes even dining plans. Check both Disneyland's official packages and offerings from third-party travel sites to compare which might offer the best value based on your needs.

FastPass and MaxPass

- **Leverage FastPass:** Utilize Disneyland's FastPass system to skip long lines for popular attractions. Planning which FastPasses to obtain as soon as you enter the park can be crucial, especially for high-demand rides.

- **Upgrade to MaxPass:** For an additional fee, Disney's MaxPass enhances your experience by allowing you to book FastPass selections via your smartphone. It also includes unlimited digital downloads of PhotoPass photos. This is particularly useful for covering more attractions with less wait time and for capturing memories without extra hassle.

Special Experiences

- **Book Special Experiences Early:** If you're interested in special experiences like guided tours, character experiences, or seasonal parties, book these as early as possible. These experiences are popular and have limited availability.

- **Check for Updates:** Always keep an eye on Disneyland's official website or app for the latest information on park hours, reservation availability, and any potential changes to services or offerings.

Implementing these booking strategies can make your Disneyland visit smoother and more enjoyable. By planning, utilizing the right tools, and understanding what the park has to offer, you can create a truly magical experience tailored just for you and your family.

Tips for Purchasing Tickets in Advance

When planning a trip to Disneyland, purchasing tickets in advance is not just a convenience—it's a necessity. Advance ticket purchases can influence everything from your entry into the park to your overall experience, especially during peak times. Here are comprehensive tips to ensure that buying your Disneyland tickets is seamless and strategic, allowing you to maximize your visit to the happiest place on Earth.

Different Ticket Options

Disneyland offers a variety of ticket types, and understanding the specifics of each is crucial:

- **Single-Day vs. Multi-Day Tickets:** Single-day tickets are good for one day's entry into one or both parks, depending on whether you purchase a Park Hopper ticket. Multi-day tickets, available for two days and up, can offer a better value per day and give you more time to explore the parks at a relaxed pace.

- **Park Hopper Tickets:** These tickets allow you to visit both Disneyland Park and Disney California Adventure on the same day. While more expensive, they offer the flexibility to move between parks, which can be particularly useful if one park reaches capacity or has longer wait times for attractions.

- **Annual Passes:** For those who plan multiple visits in a year, an annual pass might be the most cost-effective option. Evaluate how often you plan to visit to determine if this upfront investment will save you money in the long run.

Best Time to Buy Tickets

- **Purchase Well in Advance:** Especially if you're visiting during peak season (summer, holidays, and special event days), purchasing tickets as early as possible is advisable. This secures your admission and often means better pricing, as ticket prices can increase closer to the date.

- **Watch for Special Offers:** Throughout the year, Disneyland may offer special promotional pricing for residents of certain states, military personnel, or during off-peak times. Signing up for Disneyland's newsletter or following them on social media can keep you informed about these offers.

- **Group Discounts:** If traveling in a large group, check if you qualify for any group discounts. This could apply to family reunions, company trips, or school outings.

Planning Your Purchase

- **Choose Your Dates Carefully:** Before purchasing, check the Disneyland crowd calendar to pick dates with traditionally lower attendance. Visiting on less crowded days can significantly enhance your experience, allowing you more leisure time at attractions and less time waiting in lines.

- **Use Trusted Sources:** Always buy tickets directly from the Disneyland website or authorized resellers. This ensures your tickets are valid and protects you from potential scams.

- **Consider Travel Packages:** Sometimes, packages that include hotel accommodations, tickets, and sometimes dining plans can offer savings. Compare these packages from both Disneyland's official site and reputable travel agencies.

Making the Most of Your Tickets

- **Early Park Admission:** Some tickets and packages offer Extra Magic Hours or a similar benefit, allowing you early entry into the parks. This can be a critical advantage, giving you access to popular rides with minimal wait time.

- **Utilize Disneyland's Reservation System:** With the current requirement for park reservations alongside tickets, ensure you make your park reservations as soon as you purchase your tickets. This is particularly important for visits during peak times when certain dates may sell out.

- **Stay Informed:** After purchasing your tickets, keep an eye on any changes to park policies, operating hours, or health and safety guidelines. Disneyland's app and official website are excellent resources for up-to-date information.

Additional Tips

- **Non-Refundable Tickets:** Be aware that most Disneyland tickets are non-refundable. Be sure of your dates and plans before making a purchase.

- **Download the Disneyland App:** After purchasing your tickets, download the Disneyland app. It's an essential tool for making FastPass selections, checking wait times, navigating the parks, and even ordering food.

By following these tips for purchasing Disneyland tickets in advance, you can ensure that your visit is well-planned, stress-free, and filled with all the magic that Disney has to offer. Whether it's your first visit or your hundredth, a little planning can go a long way in creating a memorable experience.

Utilizing Disney's Genie+ System to Skip Lines

Disneyland's introduction of the Genie+ service revolutionized the way visitors experience the parks. This paid service, an evolution of the former FastPass system, allows guests to maximize their time and minimize their wait at popular attractions. For those planning a trip to Disneyland, understanding and effectively utilizing the Genie+ system can be a game-changer in navigating the park efficiently. Here's a comprehensive guide on how to make the most out of the Genie+ service during your Disneyland visit.

Understanding Genie+

Genie+ is a paid service that guests can add to their Disneyland ticket, offering the ability to book access to Lightning Lanes (formerly known as FastPass lanes) at select attractions. This service also includes additional features like Disney PhotoPass downloads, which offer unlimited digital downloads of photo content captured at the park on the day of service.

How to Purchase and Use Genie+

- **Purchase:** You can add Genie+ to your admission ticket through the Disneyland app once you enter the park. It is available for purchase on the day of your visit and cannot be bought in advance.

- **Booking Lightning Lane Selections:** Once you have purchased Genie+, you can start making Lightning Lane selections. You can make your first selection as soon as you enter the park, and after you redeem your initial selection or the arrival window passes, you can make another selection.

- **Strategic Selections:** Prioritize high-demand attractions early in the day. Attractions like Radiator Springs Racers or Star Wars: Rise of the Resistance are incredibly popular, and Lightning Lane reservations can fill up quickly.

- **Utilize the App:** The Disneyland app is integral to using Genie+. It allows you to book Lightning Lane entries, provides real-time updates on wait times, and helps you navigate the park more efficiently.

Maximizing Your Day with Genie+

- **Early Park Entry:** Arrive at the park before opening to make the most of lower crowd levels in the morning. This is especially beneficial for making your initial Genie+ selections before the queues build up.

- **Plan Your Route:** Be strategic about the order of your Lightning Lane selections based on their locations to minimize backtracking. Planning your route can save significant time and energy.

- **Keep Booking:** Continue to book Lightning Lane entries throughout the day. After you use a Lightning Lane, immediately book the next one. Stay aware of the rules, as you can typically hold one Lightning Lane reservation at a time, but sometimes you can book another one to two hours after the previous booking if the next available time is delayed.

Additional Tips for Using Genie+

- **Pair with Standby Lines:** Mix your use of Genie+ Lightning Lane selections with standby lines during off-peak times for less popular attractions. This strategy allows you to make the most of your day, balancing between waiting in shorter standby lines and skipping longer ones via Lightning Lanes.

- **Monitor App Notifications:** Keep notifications on for the Disneyland app. It can alert you to new availability or changes in reservation times, helping you adjust your plans on the fly.

- **Use During Peak Times:** Genie+ is most valuable during peak visitor times and on busy days. If you visit during an off-peak period, the benefit of Genie+ might not be as significant, so assess the crowd levels upon arrival to decide if it's worth the purchase that day.

- **Review Experiences:** Some experiences and attractions do not offer Lightning Lane access or may not be worth using Genie+ for. Review the list of attractions included with Genie+ beforehand and plan which ones you intend to prioritize.

Best Practices for Dining Reservations

Dining at Disneyland is not just a matter of refueling between attractions; it's an integral part of the experience, offering a variety of culinary delights that cater to every taste and preference. To make the most of dining opportunities and avoid the disappointment of long waits or missed experiences, securing reservations at Disneyland's restaurants is a key strategy. Here are best practices for making dining reservations, ensuring a seamless and enjoyable dining experience during your Disneyland visit.

Understand the Dining Options

Disneyland boasts a wide array of dining venues, from quick-service spots that require no reservations to high-demand table-service restaurants that can book up weeks in advance. Before your visit, familiarize yourself with the different options:

- **Table-Service Restaurants:** These locations, like the Blue Bayou and Carthay Circle Restaurant, offer full-service dining experiences and are extremely popular. Reservations are almost always necessary.

- **Quick-Service Restaurants:** For a more casual or speedy meal, these eateries do not require reservations. However, using mobile orders through the Disneyland app can save you time.

- **Character Dining:** Meals at these venues include visits from Disney characters. These experiences are perfect for families and are available at several restaurants around the park and hotels. Reservations are essential.

Reserve in Advance

The most important tip for ensuring your choice of Disneyland dining is to book as early as possible:

- **Reservation Window:** You can make dining reservations up to 60 days in advance. Mark this date on your calendar and be ready to book right when the window opens, especially if you are visiting during peak times or want a reservation for a particularly popular restaurant.

- **Flexibility:** If your first choice isn't available, be flexible with dates and times. Sometimes, shifting your mealtime by just an hour or picking a different day can open up availability.

- **Large Groups:** If you're traveling with a large party, make reservations as early as possible, as accommodating big groups can be challenging, particularly at smaller venues.

Utilize Technology

Leverage technology to enhance your dining experience at Disneyland:

- **Disneyland App:** This app is crucial for both making reservations and adjusting them on the go. You can also check menu options and see current restaurant hours.

- **Mobile Ordering:** For quick-service restaurants, use the app's mobile order feature to order food in advance and skip the regular lines, saving valuable time.

Plan Around Your Schedule

Coordinate your dining plans with your overall park itinerary:

- **Meal Timing:** Consider how meal times can fit into your day's schedule. For example, booking a dinner around parade times might mean you get a seat with a view of the parade route at certain restaurants.

- **Park Hopping:** If you plan to visit more than one park in a day, consider where you will be around meal times and book restaurants accordingly to avoid unnecessary back-and-forth travel.

Special Requests and Considerations

Accommodate any special dietary needs or celebrations:

- **Dietary Restrictions:** Disneyland restaurants are accommodating various dietary needs, from allergies to specific diet plans like vegan or gluten-free. Mention any dietary restrictions when making your reservation and again to your server at the restaurant.

- **Celebrations:** If you're celebrating a special occasion, note that when making your reservation. Some locations may offer celebration acknowledgments such as a special dessert or greeting.

Keep Checking Back

If you didn't get your desired reservation:

- **Regularly Check for Cancellations:** Plans change, and sometimes reservations open up. Keep checking, especially a few days before your intended dining date, as this is when most people finalize their plans and cancellations happen.

- **Walk-Up List:** Some restaurants have day-of availability via a walk-up list on the Disneyland app. This feature can be a great last-minute option.

Planning your dining experiences at Disneyland can significantly enhance your visit, turning meal times into memorable highlights of your trip. By booking ahead, using the available technology wisely, and planning your meals strategically around your park itinerary, you can enjoy a seamless and delightful dining experience. Whether you're looking for a quick bite or a sumptuous sit-down meal, a little planning goes a long way in the lively environment of Disneyland.

Chapter 3

Hidden Gems in the Park

While Disneyland is renowned for its iconic attractions like the thrilling Space Mountain and the enchanting Sleeping Beauty Castle, the park is also sprinkled with numerous hidden gems that often escape the average visitor's notice. These lesser-known attractions, quiet nooks, and unique experiences offer a delightful escape from the big crowds and a chance to explore Disneyland's quieter side.

Venturing beyond the well-trodden paths of Disneyland reveals a landscape rich with hidden experiences and secret delights.

Whether it's a secluded garden perfect for a midday respite or an overlooked attraction that offers its own unique charm, these hidden gems enhance the Disneyland experience by offering a sense of discovery and personal space amidst the excitement of the park.

Discovering the Overlooked

Many of Disneyland's hidden gems come in the form of attractions that don't feature the typical fanfare or long lines. These might include smaller, interactive exhibits, quiet thematic corners, or even historical markers that tell the deep, often overlooked stories of the park's origins and evolution. For those who take pleasure in the details and the stories behind the scenes, these elements can provide a rainbow of entertainment.

Peaceful Retreats

In every themed land, there are pockets of tranquility where one can take a moment to relax and enjoy the ambiance away from the crowd. These might be beautifully themed seating areas, lesser-known short walking paths, or architectural features that offer a quiet moment of beauty. Finding these spots often requires a bit more attention and willingness to explore off the main routes.

Unique Culinary Delights

Beyond the famous churros and Dole Whips, Disneyland hosts a variety of unique dining experiences that often go unnoticed. From hidden lounges to specialty snacks found only in obscure corners of the park, these culinary treasures offer unique flavors and a break from the typical theme park fare.

Special Experiences and Interactions

Some of the most memorable moments in Disneyland come from spontaneous character interactions or special performances that are not widely advertised. Knowing where and when to find these can transform an ordinary park day into something truly special.

As we explore these lesser-known facets of Disneyland, this chapter will guide you through not just the physical spaces but also how to enhance your visit by engaging with the park in more intimate, less crowded ways. Whether you're a first-time visitor or a seasoned Disney enthusiast, discovering these hidden gems can make your trip to Disneyland feel as if it's been tailored just for you.

Section 1

Lesser-Known Attractions

Disneyland is a treasure trove of well-known rides and attractions, but it also houses many lesser-known gems that offer delightful experiences away from the typical crowds. These attractions, often overlooked in favor of headline-grabbing rides, provide unique entertainment and a more relaxed pace, perfect for those looking to explore the park's quieter side. Here, we discover some of Disneyland's lesser-known attractions that deserve a spot on your itinerary.

The Enchanted Tiki Room

Tucked away in Adventureland, the Enchanted Tiki Room is an original feature of Disneyland, dating back to its early days. This charming show features a chorus of audio-animatronic tropical birds, flowers, and tiki statues that sing and entertain guests in a cool, dimly lit room. It's a delightful escape from the sun and a chance to experience a piece of Disney history that many guests pass by.

Sleeping Beauty Castle Walkthrough

While the Sleeping Beauty Castle itself is a prominent icon, many visitors are unaware that you can actually walk through the castle. Inside, you'll find a series of dioramas depicting the story of Sleeping Beauty, created with stunning detail. This attraction offers a quiet, self-paced exploration that provides a magical glimpse into one of Disney's beloved fairy tales.

The Animation Academy

Located in Disney California Adventure's Hollywood Land, The Animation Academy is a creative escape where guests can learn how to draw Disney characters in a classroom setting led by a professional animator. This attraction offers a personal touch and a take-home souvenir of your own making—a drawing of a Disney character guided by a Disney artist.

The Redwood Creek Challenge Trail

For those looking to stretch their legs and let their kids burn off some energy, the Redwood Creek Challenge Trail in California Adventure offers just that. This expansive outdoor play area simulates a wilderness adventure with rope bridges, slides, and climbing structures. It's often less crowded and provides a great break from the more structured attractions.

The Main Street Cinema

On Main Street, U.S.A., the Main Street Cinema offers a nostalgic trip to the early 20th century, where guests can watch classic Disney animated shorts in a quaint cinema setting. This spot is a peaceful retreat from the vibrant street outside and offers a touch of Disney magic that is often overlooked by those rushing to the bigger attractions.

The Sailing Ship Columbia

While many guests flock to the nearby Pirates of the Caribbean or the Mark Twain Riverboat, the Sailing Ship Columbia offers a unique voyage on the Rivers of America. This full-scale replica of the first American ship to circumnavigate the globe provides a detailed and immersive look at maritime life in the 18th century. The ship often has shorter wait times and offers a serene view of the park from the water.

Secret Paths and Quiet Corners

Finally, Disneyland is filled with hidden paths and quiet corners that provide not just shortcuts but also moments of tranquility. From the path running along the Rivers of America behind Big Thunder Mountain Railroad to the tucked-away seating areas near the Royal Theatre, these spots allow for peaceful pauses where you can enjoy the park's atmosphere away from the crowds.

Each of these attractions offers a unique experience, often with shorter wait times and a more relaxed environment. They exemplify the depth and richness of Disneyland, revealing that the magic of the park isn't just in its most famous rides but also in its quieter, more hidden experiences. These lesser-known attractions are perfect for those seeking a different pace or wanting to discover new aspects of the park on their return visits.

Exploring The Enchanted Tiki Room: A Peaceful Escape

Nestled in the heart of Adventureland at Disneyland, The Enchanted Tiki Room stands as a timeless homage to the magic of Disney animatronics and thematic storytelling. This attraction, often bypassed by those rushing towards more adrenaline-pumping rides, offers a unique and peaceful escape that encapsulates Walt Disney's original vision for an immersive, animated experience. As one of the first attractions to feature Audio-Animatronics technology, The Enchanted Tiki Room invites guests into a tropical paradise where the flora and fauna sing, creating an enchanting atmosphere that is both relaxing and mesmerizing.

The Historical Significance

The Enchanted Tiki Room, which opened in 1963, was the first attraction to utilize Audio-Animatronics technology in a full show, setting the stage for future innovations at Disney parks worldwide. Originally envisioned as a dinner show, it transformed into a 15-minute performance where the audience could sit back and enjoy the intricate details and pioneering animatronics surrounded by a lush, exotic setting. This attraction showcased Disney's technological ambition and his commitment to providing a diverse range of attractions that could enchant all ages.

The Attraction Experience

As you step inside The Enchanted Tiki Room, you are greeted by an array of tropical colors and the sounds of gentle, thematic music, setting the tone for a truly immersive experience. The room itself is circular, with a central fountain surrounded by rows of benches designed to give every guest an unobstructed view of the show.

The show begins as the lights dim and the cast of over 150 animatronic characters comes to life. Four host macaws, each with a distinct personality and accent, lead the performance with witty banter and song, engaging the audience with their humorous dialogue. As the show progresses, a variety of birds, flowers, and tiki statues join in, singing classic songs like "The Tiki Tiki Tiki Room" and "Let's All Sing Like the Birdies Sing," which are both whimsical and nostalgically charming.

The ceiling and walls contribute to the ambiance with stars twinkling and tropical storms simulated, adding layers of sensory immersion that captivate the audience. This atmospheric magic is enhanced by the synchronized lighting and sound effects, making the environment feel alive and dynamic.

Why It's a Must-Visit

- **A Haven of Relaxation:** In the hustle and bustle of a busy day at Disneyland, The Enchanted Tiki Room provides a welcome respite. The cool, dimly-lit room offers a comfortable place to sit and unwind, where the soothing songs and gentle movements of the animatronics provide a calming effect.

- **Cultural Celebration:** The attraction celebrates Polynesian culture and the allure of the South Seas, which was a popular aesthetic in the mid-20th century. It offers a cultural tableau that is both educational and entertaining, enriched with authentic music and folklore that pay homage to the Pacific Islands.

- **Artistic and Technological Marvel:** For enthusiasts of Disney history and animatronics, The Enchanted Tiki Room is a showcase of early technological achievement in the theme park industry. Observing these pioneering animatronics up close offers insight into the evolution of entertainment technology.

Tips for Visiting

- **Timing Your Visit:** The Enchanted Tiki Room operates continuously throughout the day, with shows typically starting every 15 to 20 minutes. Visiting during parade times or in the evening can often mean smaller audiences and a more intimate experience.

- **Interacting with Cast Members:** The cast members who introduce the show often have a wealth of knowledge about the attraction's history and details. Engaging with them can enhance your appreciation and understanding of this iconic show.

- **Exploring the Waiting Area:** Don't rush through the waiting area adorned with intricate Polynesian carvings and lush greenery. It sets the thematic tone and is an integral part of the overall experience, filled with hidden details that enhance the storyline and atmosphere.

The Enchanted Tiki Room is more than just an attraction; it is a piece of Disney history, a quiet retreat, and a celebration of imagination and innovation. For those looking to experience a different facet of Disneyland's magic, this attraction offers a perfect blend of nostalgia, tranquility, and cultural enrichment. It remains proof of Walt Disney's vision of a fully immersive entertainment experience, making it a must-visit for anyone

Introvert's Disneyland Travel for Crowd Haters   by Linus Alden Knight

---

seeking a peaceful yet profoundly enchanting escape within the lively park.

Discovering Tom Sawyer Island: A Quiet, Immersive Experience

In the center of Disneyland, amidst the thrilling rides and spectacular parades, lies a hidden retreat that echoes with the spirit of adventure and exploration—Tom Sawyer Island. This often-overlooked attraction offers a serene escape from the typical park experience, providing a unique adventure for visitors of all ages who are willing to take a brief raft ride across the Rivers of America to discover it.

The Allure of Tom Sawyer Island

Tom Sawyer Island was personally designed by Walt Disney, who was dissatisfied with the original plans and took it upon himself to redesign the entire layout. Inspired by the tales of Mark Twain, the island is a physical manifestation of the adventurous world of Tom Sawyer and Huck Finn. It's a place where the imagination can roam as freely as the paths and bridges that crisscross the landscape.

Stepping into Adventure

Upon arriving at Tom Sawyer Island, guests are transported into a lush, wooded hideaway that feels worlds apart from the rest of

Disneyland. The island is accessible only by rafts, which themselves are part of the adventure, setting the tone for an experience that feels both exclusive and exploratory.

Once ashore, visitors can wander through a variety of trails, each leading to different attractions and hidden features. The island is home to mysterious caves, rustic buildings, and elaborate play areas that encourage hands-on exploration. For children and those young at heart, it offers a chance to climb, explore, and let their imaginations lead the way.

Attractions and Hidden Gems

- **Pirate's Lair:** In 2007, the island was rebranded as Pirate's Lair on Tom Sawyer Island, incorporating elements from the "Pirates of the Caribbean" film franchise. This addition brought a pirate twist to the island's classic adventures, including treasure caves and shipwrecks that spark the thrill of piracy and discovery.

- **Injun Joe's Cave:** A labyrinth of dark, twisting pathways, and eerie sounds, this cave provides a spine-tingling adventure for those brave enough to enter. The cave's design cleverly uses darkness and narrow passages to amplify its mysterious atmosphere.

- **Fort Wilderness:** Reconstructed after being closed for several years, this fort offers panoramic views of the island and the surrounding river. It's a great spot for kids to play and adults to take a moment to appreciate the quieter side of Disneyland.

- **Smuggler's Cove:** A complex of suspension bridges and barrel bridges, Smuggler's Cove is a physically engaging area where visitors can interact with their environment, manipulating pulleys and levers to create water effects and sounds.

The Experience of Solitude and Exploration

One of the unique aspects of Tom Sawyer Island is its capacity to provide solitude amid Disneyland's often crowded environs. The design of the island—with its nooks, crannies, and secluded spots—allows visitors to find their little piece of tranquility, whether it's beside a quiet stream or under the shade of an ancient oak.

The island also offers a truly immersive experience, encouraging visitors to engage with their surroundings in a direct, physical way that is rare in modern theme parks. This tactile engagement, combined with the island's rich theming, makes every visit feel like a genuine adventure.

Tips for Visiting Tom Sawyer Island

- **Best Times to Visit:** The island opens later and closes earlier than the rest of the park, so plan to visit during midday or early afternoon. Check the daily schedule, as operations can be affected by weather or seasonal changes.

- **Prepare for Physical Activity:** Wear comfortable shoes and be prepared for a fair amount of walking. The terrain can be uneven, and the caves and forts require some ducking and climbing.

- **Bring Snacks and Water:** There are few amenities available on the island, so bringing water and a light snack can make your visit more enjoyable, especially on hot days.

- **Enjoy at Your Own Pace**: Don't rush your exploration. The charm of Tom Sawyer Island lies in its ability to transport you to a world of yesteryear adventures. Take your time to enjoy all the details and hidden corners.

Tom Sawyer Island remains one of Disneyland's hidden gems, offering a unique blend of adventure, tranquility, and nostalgia. It's a must-visit for those looking to step off the beaten path and experience a different side of the Magic Kingdom—a side where the spirit of exploration and the joy of discovery are alive and well. For anyone seeking a quieter, more immersive experience, Tom Sawyer Island promises a delightful escape, rich with the magic that only Disneyland can provide.

Enjoying The Many Adventures of Winnie the Pooh: Short Lines and Charm

Nestled in the whimsical corner of Disneyland's Critter Country, The Many Adventures of Winnie the Pooh stands as a colorful and enchanting attraction, often overshadowed by its more thrilling counterparts. This delightful ride offers a serene escape into the Hundred Acre Wood, home of the beloved Pooh bear and his friends. With typically short lines and a heartwarming storyline, this attraction provides a perfect blend of nostalgia and charm for guests of all ages.

The Magic of Hundred Acre Wood

The Many Adventures of Winnie the Pooh ride is a vibrant ride through a series of vignettes that bring to life A.A. Milne's classic tales. Opened in 2003, the ride replaced the Country Bear Jamboree but has since carved its own niche in the hearts of Disney guests. As you board your "hunny" pot and set off on the adventure, you're immediately immersed in the storybook world, where friendship and imagination reign.

A Ride Through Pooh's Adventures

The ride begins with a friendly greeting from Pooh Bear himself, setting the stage for a series of delightful scenes. Guests are taken through blustery days, bouncy escapades with Tigger, a surreal dream sequence with Heffalumps and Woozles, and a rainy rescue that culminates in a grand celebration. Each scene is meticulously crafted with vibrant colors, dynamic effects, and animatronics that bring the characters to life.

Immersive Storytelling

One of the standout features of this ride is its immersive storytelling. The narrative is easy to follow, making it particularly appealing to younger visitors or those unfamiliar with thrill rides. The gentle movements of the ride vehicles and the engaging audio make it accessible and enjoyable for families with small children or guests looking for a calming diversion.

Charming Details

Disney's attention to detail is evident throughout the ride. From the depiction of Pooh stuck in Rabbit's hole to the playful interaction with Tigger, every element is designed to enhance the sense of whimsy and joy. The backgrounds and settings are rich with elements from the books, providing a visual feast that rewards repeat visits.

Benefits of Short Wait Times

A significant advantage of The Many Adventures of Winnie the Pooh is the typically shorter wait times compared to more popular attractions like Splash Mountain or the Haunted Mansion. This accessibility allows guests to enjoy the ride multiple times during their visit or to use it as a pleasant respite between more crowded experiences.

Ideal for All Ages

The ride's gentle nature and captivating visuals make it ideal for guests of all ages. It's particularly suitable for families with young children, providing a safe and engaging experience that can serve as an introduction to Disneyland rides. For older guests, the nostalgic appeal of Winnie the Pooh and the Hundred Acre Wood offers a charming return to the beloved stories of their childhood.

Tips for Visiting

- **Best Times to Ride:** While wait times for this attraction are generally shorter, visiting during parade times or evening hours can provide an even more relaxed experience.

- **Exploring Critter Country:** Pair your visit to Pooh's adventure with other attractions in Critter Country, such as Splash Mountain and the nearby dining spots, to make the most of this quieter corner of the park.

- **Look for Hidden Details:** Keep an eye out for hidden details throughout the ride, including a tribute to the Country Bear Jamboree in one of the final scenes. These

Easter eggs add an extra layer of enjoyment for Disney aficionados.

- **Photo Opportunities:** The ride exits into Pooh's Corner, a themed shop where you can often meet Pooh and his friends for photos. This is a wonderful opportunity to capture memories of the day, especially for young fans.

The Many Adventures of Winnie the Pooh offers a delightful escape into a world of nostalgia, friendship, and imagination. Its shorter lines and immersive charm make it a must-visit for anyone looking for a more relaxed and enchanting experience at Disneyland.

Section 2

Serene Spots for Relaxation

Disneyland, renowned for its lively atmosphere and thrills, also harbors several serene spots perfect for relaxation and a peaceful respite from the excitement. These quieter nooks offer a moment of calm and tranquility, allowing guests to recharge before continuing their adventure-filled day.

The Quiet Charm of New Orleans Square

One of Disneyland's most beautifully themed areas, New Orleans Square, is not just home to popular attractions like Pirates of the Caribbean and the Haunted Mansion. It also offers charming courtyards and secluded pathways where one can escape the crowds. The French Market Restaurant, with its covered seating area, provides a pleasant, shaded environment where guests can enjoy a meal or a drink while listening to the distant sounds of live jazz music. Nearby, the Court of Angels, a lesser-known gem within the square, offers a quiet stairwell adorned with beautiful wrought iron that is perfect for reflection or a restful break.

The Gardens Around the Disneyland Hub

The central hub of Disneyland, located at the end of Main Street, U.S.A., near the iconic Sleeping Beauty Castle, features a series of intricately landscaped gardens. Each garden around the hub offers a unique floral display and bench seating, providing a picturesque setting for relaxation. These areas are particularly delightful during off-peak hours, when you can enjoy the beauty of the flowers and the iconic view of the castle with fewer interruptions.

The Shaded Retreats of Adventureland

Adventureland, known for its dense foliage and exotic theming, hosts several hidden spots ideal for a quiet break. Behind the Tiki

Room, guests can find a secluded area filled with tropical plants that are often missed by the crowds. This spot offers a cool, quiet place to enjoy a snack or simply sit and relax amid the lush greenery. Additionally, the area around the Jungle Cruise, with its covered queue and atmospheric jungle sounds, provides a pseudo-retreat where one can immerse in the ambiance of a distant land.

The Secluded Benches of Critter Country

Critter Country, located at the far end of the park, is often less crowded than other areas. Here, guests can find peaceful retreats near the Davy Crockett Explorer Canoes and along the banks of the Rivers of America. The area offers numerous benches under the shade of tall trees, perfect for taking a moment to unwind. The nearby Hungry Bear Restaurant also features upper and lower deck seating with serene views of the river, ideal for a quiet meal away from the park's busier paths.

The Tranquil Paths of Tom Sawyer Island

As previously mentioned, Tom Sawyer Island offers an array of adventures and also acts as a tranquil getaway with its quiet paths and hidden caves. Accessible only by raft, this island serves as a serene escape with spots like Injun Joe's Cave, where the cool, dimly lit interiors provide a respite from the sun, and the breezy mill, where one can sit and watch the river flow by.

Relaxing in Mickey's Toontown

Mickey's Toontown, typically crowded with energy and laughter, also contains quieter areas designed for relaxation. Near the very back of Toontown, past the cartoonish cityscape, is a lesser-known garden area with seating. It's a colorful and cheerful place where guests can take a breather and let younger visitors play in a less crowded setting.

Finding Peace in The Royal Street Veranda: Great Snacks with Fewer Crowds

Nestled in the heart of New Orleans Square at Disneyland, The Royal Street Veranda offers a quaint and often overlooked retreat for guests seeking a peaceful snack break away from the heavy crowds. Known for its delicious menu and serene ambiance, this spot combines the charm of New Orleans with the magic of Disney, providing a unique dining experience that can be a quiet respite during a busy day at the park.

The Charm of New Orleans Square

The Royal Street Veranda is tucked away in a less-trafficked part of New Orleans Square, situated just off the path that many rush along to reach popular attractions like Pirates of the Caribbean and the Haunted Mansion. The area embodies the essence of a lazy afternoon in the French Quarter, complete with intricate ironwork balconies and the soft murmur of jazz drifting through the air. This setting enhances the dining experience and transports guests to a different world, away from the typical theme park hustle.

Culinary Delights at The Royal Street Veranda

The menu at The Royal Street Veranda is best known for its savory soups served in hearty sourdough bread bowls, a perfect comforting meal for any time of the day. The selection typically includes classics such as New England clam chowder, hearty vegetarian gumbo, and the rich, flavorful steak gumbo. Each dish is prepared with care, offering warm, nourishing options that are ideal for refueling after exploring the park.

Aside from its famous soups, the Veranda also serves a variety of snacks and beverages. Guests can enjoy a selection of coffees and specialty drinks, which make for a perfect pick-me-up during a mid-afternoon lull. The snack options, though simpler, are crafted to provide quick and satisfying bites for those on the go.

A Quiet Nook for Dining

One of the main draws of The Royal Street Veranda is its relatively hidden location and the calm atmosphere it offers. Unlike more prominent eateries around the park, this spot often has shorter lines and plenty of seating. The dining area, shaded and adorned with plants, overlooks some of the quieter walkways of New Orleans Square, providing a picturesque view that complements the meal.

The architecture and decor reflect the quaint charm of New Orleans, with details that echo the historic antebellum style. Guests can take their time to enjoy their meals without feeling rushed, making it a perfect spot for those looking to take a break from the day's activities and soak in the ambiance of one of Disneyland's most thematic areas.

Tips for Visiting the Royal Street Veranda

- **Visit During Off-Peak Hours:** For the most peaceful experience, try to visit during off-peak times, such as late morning or mid-afternoon, when most guests are either starting their day or heading to major attractions.

- **Enjoy the Scenery:** After picking up your food, take a moment to explore the surrounding area. The nearby balconies, hidden alcoves, and intricate details offer a delightful backdrop for a leisurely meal.

- **Pair Your Visit with Nearby Attractions:** Plan your meal around a visit to adjacent attractions. Enjoying a quieter meal at the Veranda can be a strategic stop before heading to the busier rides, allowing for a well-timed break in your day.

- **Check for Seasonal Offerings:** The Royal Street Veranda occasionally updates its menu with seasonal specials or new flavors, especially during special events or holidays at Disneyland. Checking the menu beforehand or asking cast members about any new offerings can enhance your dining experience.

Quiet Seating Areas Throughout the Park

While Disneyland is famously crowded and vibrant, there are numerous quiet seating areas scattered throughout the park where visitors can find a moment of peace. These spots offer a welcome respite from the constant activity, providing spaces to relax, enjoy a snack, or simply take in the surroundings. Whether you're looking for a shady bench to rest your feet or a secluded area to regroup with your family, Disneyland has several options to consider.

Main Street, U.S.A. - Central Plaza

At the end of Main Street, U.S.A., just before the iconic Sleeping Beauty Castle, lies the Central Plaza. This area offers several benches under well-manicured trees, providing a picturesque view of the castle while escaping the main thoroughfare's hustle and bustle. The Central Plaza is particularly pleasant during parade times when most guests are lined up along the parade route, leaving the benches less crowded.

Adventureland - Aladdin's Oasis

Tucked away in Adventureland, Aladdin's Oasis used to be a lively snack spot but now serves as a quiet seating area where guests can relax amid Middle Eastern architectural decor. This hidden nook is shaded and beautifully themed, making it a charming spot to unwind and enjoy the ambient sounds of nearby attractions like the Jungle Cruise.

New Orleans Square - French Market Restaurant

The French Market Restaurant in New Orleans Square offers a spacious dining area with both indoor and outdoor seating. The outdoor section, covered by large umbrellas and surrounded by lush plants, provides a cooler, quieter dining experience away from the crowds. After grabbing a meal or a drink here, you can enjoy a peaceful break while listening to the distant jazz music that characterizes this part of the park.

Critter Country - Hungry Bear Restaurant

At the very back of Critter Country, the lower deck of the Hungry Bear Restaurant overlooks the Rivers of America. This location is usually less crowded and offers a peaceful view of the water, making it an ideal spot for those looking to enjoy a quiet meal or simply sit back and relax in a serene setting.

Fantasyland - Small World Promenade

Adjacent to the "it's a small world" attraction, the Small World Promenade features a number of benches and a less trafficked pathway that offers a peaceful escape from Fantasyland's usual chaos. This area is especially quiet during the first parade of the day when most of the crowd is watching the parade elsewhere.

Frontierland - Fowler's Harbor

This small, often overlooked area near the entrance to the Pirate's Lair on Tom Sawyer Island is a quaint spot to sit and relax. Fowler's Harbor provides benches with a view of the sailing ship Columbia or the Mark Twain Riverboat, offering a quiet, picturesque place to take a break from the park's more energetic activities.

Tomorrowland - Near Autopia

Behind the busy pathways near the Autopia ride, there are several benches where you can sit and enjoy a quieter side of Tomorrowland. This area is less frequented by guests and provides a space where you can watch the monorail quietly pass by overhead, offering a futuristic yet peaceful backdrop.

Tips for Finding Quiet Spots

- **Explore Off-Peak Hours:** Many of these quiet areas become even more peaceful during the early morning hours or late evening, just before the park closes.

- **Use the Disneyland App:** The app can help you find locations throughout the park and check live wait times, allowing you to strategically plan when to visit busier areas and when to retreat to quieter ones.

- **Be Observant:** Often, the best quiet spots are discovered simply by exploring or noticing where the crowds aren't. Don't be afraid to venture down less populated pathways or explore areas behind main attractions.

Finding these quiet seating areas in Disneyland can greatly enhance your visit, allowing for moments of rest and relaxation amidst a day filled with excitement and adventure.

The Beauty of Disneyland's Gardens: Ideal for Reflection and Rest

While Disneyland is celebrated for its thrilling rides and enchanting characters, it is also home to beautifully curated gardens that offer peaceful sanctuaries throughout the park. These gardens enhance the aesthetic appeal of Disneyland and provide ideal spots for reflection, rest, and respite from the heavy crowd. Each garden, meticulously designed and maintained, reflects the themes of its surroundings and invites guests to pause and appreciate the quieter beauty of nature amidst the magic of Disneyland.

Main Street, U.S.A. - The Hub

At the heart of Disneyland, just before the iconic Sleeping Beauty Castle, lies the Hub. This central area features a series of radiating pathways lined with manicured lawns, vibrant flower beds, and mature trees. The Hub's garden is particularly striking during seasonal changes when the floral arrangements are redesigned to match the festivities, from bright tulips in spring to rich chrysanthemums in the fall. Benches and lamp posts dot the landscape, providing spots to sit and enjoy the view of the castle, often accompanied by the sound of a live band playing classic Disney tunes.

New Orleans Square - The Courtyards

The gardens in New Orleans Square are among the most intricately themed areas within Disneyland. Hidden behind the busy streets, you'll find quiet courtyards filled with Southern charm, featuring magnolia trees, creeping figs, and blooming flowers that seem to transport you directly to Louisiana. The fragrant smells and the soft sound of jazz floating through the air make these courtyards a delightful escape for those seeking a moment of tranquility.

Fantasyland - Snow White's Grotto

On the side of the Sleeping Beauty Castle, Snow White's Grotto offers a whimsical garden setting that is both enchanting and serene. This area features a wishing well, a small waterfall, and statues of Snow White and the Seven Dwarfs, all surrounded by lush greenery and flowering plants. The sound of chirping birds and cascading water complements the peaceful ambiance, making it a magical spot for guests to make a wish or simply enjoy a quiet moment.

Tomorrowland - Tomorrowland Terrace

Although Tomorrowland is often associated with its futuristic attractions and dynamic energy, the Tomorrowland Terrace area presents a contrasting calmness with its shaded seating and plant-covered trellises. This garden space is functional and futuristic, with clean lines and geometric plant designs that reflect the land's theme. It's a cool, quiet place to enjoy a break, especially in the heat of the day.

Frontierland - Big Thunder Mountain Railroad

Adjacent to the Big Thunder Mountain Railroad, there's a less-visited garden area that offers a different perspective on the rugged, wild terrain of Frontierland. This area features drought-resistant landscaping that includes native plants and cacti, reflecting the gold rush and pioneer spirit of the Old West. Seating around this garden allows for restful breaks where guests can enjoy the less manicured, more natural side of Disneyland's flora.

Adventureland - The Jungle Cruise Landscaping

The landscaping around the Jungle Cruise is designed to immerse guests in a lush, tropical environment, replicating a remote jungle. This area is a visual treat and a horticultural one, featuring exotic plants from around the world that thrive in Southern California's climate. The dense foliage provides natural shade and cooling spots, ideal for guests looking to step away from the sun and immerse themselves in the sounds and sights of a tropical paradise.

Tips for Enjoying Disneyland's Gardens

- **Take a Guided Tour:** Disneyland offers guided tours that sometimes focus on the landscaping and botanical aspects of the park. These can provide deeper insights into the design and care of Disneyland's gardens.

- **Plan for Rest Breaks:** Incorporate stops at these garden spots into your daily itinerary, using them as peaceful breaks between the more high-energy attractions.

- **Capture the Seasons:** If you visit Disneyland more than once a year, take the time to notice how the gardens change with the seasons. Each visit can offer a new perspective and different blooms to enjoy.

- **Early Mornings or Late Evenings**: These times typically offer quieter moments to enjoy the gardens, as most guests are either starting their day with rides or heading out of the park.

Disneyland's gardens are a feast for the eyes and provide soul-soothing spots for guests to relax and reflect. These landscaped areas underscore the park's commitment to beauty and tranquility, offering peaceful havens where magic and nature meet.

Chapter 4

Navigating Popular Attractions

Disneyland is a world-renowned theme park celebrated not just for its enchanting atmosphere and storytelling prowess but also for its diverse array of thrilling and immersive attractions. From the adrenaline-pumping drops of Splash Mountain to the futuristic explorations of Space Mountain, the park offers something for everyone.

However, navigating these popular attractions can be a daunting task, especially during peak visitation times when lines can stretch and wait times soar. This chapter is designed to help you efficiently explore these popular sites, ensuring you maximize your time and enjoyment without the stress often associated with crowded theme parks.

Plan Your Strategy

A successful visit to Disneyland's most popular attractions begins long before you set foot in the park. Planning which attractions are a must-see and understanding their locations within the park are your first steps. Mapping out a route that minimizes backtracking and keeps you moving smoothly from one attraction to the next can save you significant time.

Make Use of Technology

Disneyland's mobile app is an indispensable tool for real-time park navigation. It provides up-to-date wait times for all attractions, which can help you decide on the fly whether to head to Splash Mountain now or wait until the parade starts and the lines might shorten. The app also offers the ability to reserve FastPasses for popular attractions, allowing you to skip the regular lines at designated times.

FastPass and MaxPass

Understanding and utilizing the FastPass system is perhaps the most effective way to navigate through Disneyland's most crowded attractions. A FastPass allows you to return to an attraction within a specified one-hour window to enjoy a much shorter wait time. For an additional fee, Disneyland offers MaxPass, which enhances the FastPass system by allowing you to book FastPass directly from your smartphone. It also includes PhotoPass downloads to capture memories from your visit.

Early Mornings and Late Evenings

Timing is everything at Disneyland. Arriving early or staying late can often mean experiencing shorter lines at popular attractions. Many seasoned visitors make a beeline for the busiest rides as soon as the gates open, making the most of the first few hours when the park is still relatively quiet. Similarly, during evening hours, especially during and after the nighttime shows, many attractions see a significant decrease in wait times.

Eating Off-Peak

Another strategy to consider is dining during off-peak hours. While others are eating lunch between 11:00 AM and 2:00 PM, the lines for rides can be shorter. Planning your meal times before or after the traditional lunch and dinner hours can allow you to enjoy popular attractions while others are otherwise occupied.

Seasonal and Special Event Considerations

Certain times of the year, like holidays and summer weekends, can see increased attendance. If your schedule allows, visiting during the off-season—typically late January through March or after the summer crowds dissipate in early September—can result in a much more relaxed experience. Additionally, be aware of special events or newly opened attractions, as these can significantly affect crowd levels and distribution throughout the park.

Section 1

Timing Your Visits

Timing is a critical element in planning a successful and enjoyable trip to Disneyland, especially when it comes to navigating the park's most popular attractions. The right timing can mean the difference between enduring long lines under the hot California sun and breezing through rides with minimal wait.

Understanding Peak Times

Disneyland's crowd levels can vary dramatically throughout the day and year. Generally, the park is busiest on weekends, during school holidays, and in the summer months. Conversely, weekdays during the off-season (late winter to early spring, late fall) usually see lower attendance. By planning your visit during these quieter times, you can experience significantly shorter lines and a more relaxed atmosphere.

Morning Strategy

Arriving early at Disneyland is one of the most effective tactics for avoiding long waits. The first few hours after the park opens are often the least crowded of the day, making this the ideal time to head straight for the most popular rides. Attractions like Space Mountain, Indiana Jones Adventure, and Peter Pan's Flight can have exponentially longer waits just an hour or two after opening, so prioritizing these can save you a lot of time.

Using Magic Hours

If you are staying at a Disneyland Resort hotel, take advantage of Magic Hours—early admission to the parks. This benefit allows hotel guests access to certain parts of Disneyland or Disney California Adventure before the general public. During these times, you can enjoy even lower crowd levels, giving you a head start on the day's most sought-after attractions.

Evening Opportunities

As the day progresses, crowd patterns can shift. Many families with young children tend to leave the park in the late afternoon and evening, which can reduce wait times at many attractions. Post-firework show times are also ideal for experiencing popular rides, as many guests choose to head home after the spectacle.

Dining at Off-Peak Times

Meal times at Disneyland are predictably crowded around traditional lunch and dinner hours, typically from 11:00 AM to 2:00 PM and 5:00 PM to 7:00 PM, respectively. To avoid the rush, consider eating earlier or later than these peak times.

Breaks and Recharges

Plan for breaks during the busiest midday hours, especially if visiting during the summer when the midday heat can be intense. Use this time to enjoy indoor shows, visit less popular attractions, or simply relax in shaded or air-conditioned areas. This strategic downtime can keep you refreshed and ready to tackle more rides as the crowd thins out later in the day.

Watching the Weather and Seasonal Events

Weather can also play a significant role in planning your day. Cooler, overcast days tend to deter local visitors, which can mean fewer crowds. Conversely, be mindful of seasonal events like Halloween Time or the Christmas season, which can attract larger crowds but also offer unique experiences that are not available at other times of the year.

Best Times to Experience Star Wars: Galaxy's Edge

Star Wars: Galaxy's Edge is one of the most immersive and highly acclaimed additions to Disneyland, offering an unparalleled experience for fans of the saga and new visitors alike. Since its opening, this expansive section of the park has drawn significant attention and crowds eager to explore the distant planet of Batuu. Knowing the best times to visit can greatly enhance your experience, allowing you to fully immerse yourself in the Star Wars universe without the burden of excessive wait times. Here's how to strategically plan your adventure in Galaxy's Edge.

Crowd Patterns at Galaxy's Edge

Galaxy's Edge is designed to be an all-encompassing experience that includes rides, dining, and interactive elements. The land features major attractions like Millennium Falcon: Smugglers Run and Star Wars: Rise of the Resistance, both of which are incredibly popular and typically see higher visitor volumes. Analyzing and understanding the crowd patterns can help you decide the most effective times to visit.

Early Morning Strategy

Arriving early at Galaxy's Edge can significantly improve your experience. The first few hours after the park opening are generally the best time to visit any popular area in Disneyland, and Galaxy's Edge is no exception. During this time, you can head straight to the top attractions before the queues build up. For Rise of the Resistance, which is one of Disneyland's most in-demand rides, using the virtual queue system or joining the standby line as early as possible is crucial.

Using Boarding Groups and Virtual Queues

For attractions like Rise of the Resistance, Disneyland often utilizes a virtual queue system where guests join a boarding group through the Disneyland app. This system is only available right at the park opening and at another designated time later in the day. Successfully joining a boarding group early in the morning means you can plan your visit around your assigned time, potentially avoiding the longest waits.

Late Evening Visits

As with many parts of Disneyland, visiting Galaxy's Edge later in the evening can also be advantageous. As families with young children start to leave and nighttime entertainment begins, queue times for major attractions can decrease. The ambiance of Galaxy's Edge at night is something not to be missed; the area comes alive in a different way with lighting that enhances the immersive experience of the Star Wars universe.

Midweek Visits

Choosing to visit Disneyland and Galaxy's Edge midweek (Tuesday through Thursday) can also result in shorter lines and a less crowded experience. Weekends, holidays, and summer months typically see the highest attendance. If your schedule allows, a midweek visit can make a significant difference in your experience.

Dining and Shopping at Off-Peak Times

In addition to planning when to hit the major rides, consider visiting the shops and eateries in Galaxy's Edge during off-peak hours. Places like Oga's Cantina and the Droid Depot are extremely popular. Booking reservations for Oga's Cantina well in advance is essential, and visiting shops during typical meal times or parade/show times can mean fewer crowds and a more relaxed experience.

Watching for Seasonal and Event-based Variations

Keep an eye on Disneyland's calendar for special events or seasonal changes that might affect crowd levels. Events like Star Wars Day (May the Fourth) or new product releases in the park can draw larger crowds to Galaxy's Edge. Conversely, these times can also enhance the thematic enjoyment of your visit with special merchandise, food, and possibly character interactions.

Strategies for Enjoying Haunted Mansion Without Long Waits

The Haunted Mansion, nestled in the heart of Disneyland's New Orleans Square, is one of the park's most beloved and iconic attractions. Known for its ghostly charm and eerie but fun storyline, it draws a steady stream of visitors year-round.

However, with popularity often comes long lines. To enjoy the Haunted Mansion with minimal waiting, a strategic approach is essential. Here are some effective strategies to help you bypass the longer queues and get the most out of your visit to this classic attraction.

Visit During Off-Peak Hours

- **Early Morning or Late Evening:** Like many popular rides at Disneyland, the Haunted Mansion experiences shorter wait times during the park's opening and closing hours. Arriving early can often allow you to enjoy the ride with minimal delay, as most guests are typically heading to more adrenaline-pumping attractions first. Alternatively, visiting the mansion late in the evening, especially during or after the nighttime shows when many guests start heading home, can also prove advantageous.

Utilize Disneyland's Virtual Queue and Lightning Lane

- **Maximize FastPass and Lightning Lane Access:** Disneyland offers the Lightning Lane service (formerly FastPass), which allows guests to skip the regular queue for a more expedited experience. While the availability of

Lightning Lane for the Haunted Mansion can vary depending on the park's current operational strategy and crowd levels, utilizing this service when available can significantly reduce your waiting time.

- **Check for Virtual Queue Options:** Occasionally, Disneyland may implement a virtual queue system for highly trafficked attractions, including the Haunted Mansion, especially during peak seasons or special events like the Halloween makeover. Always check the Disneyland app for the latest queue options, which can save you from physically standing in line.

Plan Around Shows and Parades

- **Strategic Timing with Park Entertainment:** The Haunted Mansion's wait times can drop during popular parade and show times. Many guests prefer to experience these events, leaving queue lines shorter for rides. Planning to visit the Haunted Mansion during such times can be a clever way to dodge longer waits.

Visit During Special Seasons with Extended Hours

- **Halloween and Holiday Seasons:** The Haunted Mansion is particularly popular during its seasonal transformations into Haunted Mansion Holiday, starting in September and continuing through the Christmas season. While these times can attract more visitors, Disneyland also extends its hours, giving you more time in the evening to visit the attraction. Moreover, the first few weeks of these seasonal changes and January—right before the decorations come down—are typically less crowded.

Consider Weather and Weekday Visits

- **Weather Impact:** Inclement weather can be a boon for indoor attractions like the Haunted Mansion. Rainy days deter some parkgoers, which can result in shorter lines. If you don't mind the weather, this can be an excellent time to explore the mansion.

- **Weekday Visits:** Planning your Disneyland trip on a weekday (preferably Tuesday through Thursday) can also help you avoid the larger crowds typical of weekends, resulting in shorter lines for the Haunted Mansion and other attractions.

Use the Disneyland App

- **Real-Time Updates:** The Disneyland app is invaluable for planning your day effectively. It provides real-time updates on wait times for all attractions, including the Haunted Mansion. By monitoring the app throughout the day, you can decide on the spur of the moment to head to the mansion when you notice a dip in wait times.

Enjoy the Full Experience

- **Explore the Queue:** If a short wait isn't possible, remember that the Haunted Mansion's queue is part of the experience. The line winds through a beautifully themed garden with subtle details that set the story's mood, complete with cryptic tombstones and eerie sounds. This can be part of the fun, setting the stage for the spooky yet whimsical adventure that awaits inside.

By employing these strategies, you can make your visit to the Haunted Mansion more enjoyable, ensuring that you spend less time in line and more time uncovering the mysteries of this ghostly retreat.

Early Entry and Late Stays

- **Morning Magic Hours and Late Nights:** If you are staying at a Disneyland Resort hotel, take advantage of the Magic Morning or Extra Magic Hour benefits. This perk allows early access to Disneyland on select days, providing an opportunity to visit the Haunted Mansion when the park is less crowded. Similarly, staying late, as the park nears closing time, can also mean fewer guests and shorter lines for the mansion.

Be Flexible

- **Adjust Plans on the Fly:** Flexibility can be your best asset in avoiding long waits. If you notice that the Haunted Mansion has unexpectedly high wait times, consider switching your plans around. You might visit another nearby attraction, such as Pirates of the Caribbean or Splash Mountain, and return to the Haunted Mansion later when the app indicates shorter wait times.

Take Advantage of Single Rider or Rider Switch

- **Rider Options:** While the Haunted Mansion does not typically offer Single Rider lines, it does participate in the Rider Switch program. If you are visiting with small children or guests who do not wish to enter the mansion, inquire about Rider Switch. This service allows one part of your party to enjoy the ride while another part waits with the non-rider and then switches without having to re-enter the general queue.

Consider a Guided Tour

- **Behind-the-Scenes Access:** Disneyland offers guided tours that sometimes include attractions like the Haunted Mansion. These tours provide a wealth of detailed information about the attractions and also include expedited access to them. Booking a tour can enhance your understanding of the Haunted Mansion's rich history and its place in Disneyland lore, all while bypassing the regular line.

Make It a Nighttime Adventure

- **Nighttime Experience:** The Haunted Mansion offers a completely different vibe at night, with the mansion's exterior eerily lit and the ambiance enhanced by the shadows and sounds of the evening. Experiencing the mansion after dark can be a unique adventure, and often, wait times begin to decrease as families with young children head home.

By integrating these strategies into your visit, you'll optimize your time at Disneyland and enrich your experience at the Haunted Mansion.

Visiting Space Mountain During Parades or Fireworks

Space Mountain, located in Tomorrowland at Disneyland, is one of the park's most exhilarating attractions. Known for its high-speed space-themed roller coaster ride in the dark, it consistently draws large crowds and long wait times. However, one strategic way to experience Space Mountain with significantly shorter queues is by planning your visit during parade or fireworks times. This approach can enhance your ride experience with reduced wait times and adds a unique twist to your Disneyland visit.

Peak Times for Space Mountain

Space Mountain's popularity means that during normal operating hours, especially midday, wait times can be quite lengthy. The attraction is a favorite among thrill-seekers and families alike, making it one of the busiest spots in Tomorrowland. However, during parades and fireworks, many guests shift their focus toward the park's iconic entertainment offerings, resulting in fewer people in line for rides.

Benefits of Riding During Parades and Fireworks

- **Shorter Wait Times:** Many guests prioritize watching Disneyland's famous parades and fireworks shows, which typically occur in the late afternoon or evening. During these times, queues at Space Mountain often decrease significantly, making it an ideal time to enjoy one of the park's most popular attractions without the usual wait.

- **Unique Evening Experience:** Riding Space Mountain at night, especially during or right after fireworks, can enhance the overall experience. The contrast between the quiet darkness of space in the ride and the bright, festive atmosphere outside adds a thrilling dynamic to the adventure.

- **Efficient Use of Time:** By visiting Space Mountain during parades and fireworks, you can maximize your day at Disneyland. This strategy allows you to experience more attractions with minimal waiting, effectively utilizing your time in the park.

Planning Your Visit

- **Check the Schedule:** Before your visit, check the Disneyland schedule for parade and fireworks timings. This information can help you plan your day around these events, ensuring you're at Space Mountain during one of these less busy times.

- **Use the Disneyland App:** The Disneyland app is invaluable for real-time updates on wait times and ride closures. Keep an eye on the app throughout the day, and be ready to head to Space Mountain when you notice a drop in wait times during the parade or fireworks preparations.

- **Consider Multiple Visits:** If the parade and fireworks schedules allow, you might be able to catch Space Mountain with reduced wait times more than once. For example, attending the first parade and then heading to

Space Mountain during the second showing of fireworks can offer back-to-back opportunities with shorter queues.

Tips for an Optimal Experience

- **Prepare for Outdoor Conditions:** If you're waiting to enter Space Mountain during a fireworks show, be prepared for cooler evening temperatures. Bringing a light jacket or sweater can make the wait more comfortable if you find yourself in a part of the queue that's exposed to the outside.

- **Enjoy the Atmosphere:** Riding Space Mountain during or just after the fireworks can add to the day's excitement. The energy from the fireworks show tends to carry over into the ride, enhancing the exhilaration of the roller coaster.

- **Stay Safe:** Navigating the park during parade and fireworks times, especially in the dark, requires extra caution. Keep your group together, watch for parade route barriers, and be mindful of the increased crowd movements during these times.

- **Use FastPass or MaxPass Wisely:** If available, securing a FastPass or MaxPass reservation for Space Mountain right before or during a parade or fireworks show can further reduce your wait time. This can be especially beneficial if the regular queue is still longer than expected.

Visiting Space Mountain during Disneyland's parades or fireworks presents a strategic opportunity to enjoy one of the park's top attractions with fewer crowds and shorter wait times.

This approach allows you to experience the thrill of Space Mountain in a unique setting and helps you optimize your overall visit to Disneyland, ensuring that every minute at the park is filled with magic and adventure.

Section 2

Smart Approaches

Successfully navigating Disneyland's popular attractions requires more than just luck; it demands strategic planning and smart approaches. By understanding the park's layout, utilizing available technology, and incorporating a few insider tips, you can enhance your experience, minimize wait times, and enjoy more of what Disneyland has to offer.

Using the Disneyland App

The Disneyland app is a critical tool for any visitor. It provides real-time information on ride wait times, show schedules, and even restaurant menus. Use the app to:

- **Monitor Wait Times:** Keep an eye on the app throughout your visit to stay updated on fluctuating wait times. This can help you decide when to head to popular rides like Space Mountain or Indiana Jones Adventure.

- **Mobile Ordering:** Use the app to order mobile food and beverages from various park restaurants. This can save you valuable time that would otherwise be spent standing in line.

- **Access Virtual Queues and Lightning Lane:** Some of Disneyland's most popular rides, like Star Wars: Rise of the Resistance, use virtual queues and Lightning Lane selections available through the app. Familiarize yourself with these features to take full advantage.

Planning Your Route

Efficient navigation through Disneyland can significantly reduce unnecessary walking and waiting. Plan your route through the park by:

- **Grouping Attractions:** Focus on one area of the park at a time. This minimizes backtracking and helps you cover more ground with less effort.

- **Starting at the Back:** Upon park opening, head towards the attractions furthest from the entrance. Many guests stop at the first rides they encounter, so by starting at the back, you can enjoy shorter early-morning lines.

Timing Your Visits to Attractions

Time management is key in a venue as large and popular as Disneyland. Consider these timing strategies:

- **Arrive Early:** Being at the gates before the park opens can give you a head-start on the day. Head straight to the rides that typically have the longest lines during the day.

- **Leverage Parades and Shows:** During parades and fireworks, many guests are occupied, leading to shorter lines for rides. Plan to visit high-demand attractions during these times.

- **Use Rider Switch:** If you're visiting with small children, take advantage of Disneyland's Rider Switch service, which allows one parent to ride while the other waits with the child, then switch without waiting in the regular line again.

Dining Strategically

Meal times can also impact your day at Disneyland, especially if you spend waiting in long lines for food. Use these dining strategies:

- **Off-Peak Dining**: Eat meals during off-peak hours. Plan to have lunch before 11:30 AM or after 2 PM and dinner before 5 PM or after 7 PM.

- **Character Breakfasts:** If you're interested in character dining experiences, book a character breakfast. These meals provide a fun and interactive way to meet characters without taking time away from riding attractions.

Rest and Recovery

Don't underestimate the importance of rest:

- **Scheduled Breaks:** Schedule breaks throughout your day, especially if visiting with children. Find quiet spots or return to your hotel in the afternoon for a rest.

- **Stay Hydrated and Protected:** Drink plenty of water and wear sunscreen. Keeping yourself hydrated and protected from the sun helps maintain energy levels throughout the day.

Being Flexible

Finally, while a plan is invaluable, flexibility can often be just as crucial. Be prepared to modify your plans based on real-time information, unexpected opportunities, or simply how you and your group are feeling. Sometimes, spontaneous decisions lead to some of the most memorable moments at Disneyland.

By adopting these smart approaches, you can ensure that your visit to Disneyland is magical and efficient, allowing you to make the most of your time in this enchanting world.

How to Use Single Rider Lines Effectively

Disneyland offers a variety of ways to enjoy its attractions, including the often-overlooked single-rider lines. These lines are designed to fill empty seats that occur when groups don't occupy all the available spots on a ride, and they can significantly reduce your wait time. Understanding how to use single-rider lines effectively can enhance your visit by allowing you to experience more rides in less time.

Single Rider Lines

Single-rider lines are available at several Disneyland attractions, including popular rides like Indiana Jones Adventure, Radiator Springs Racers, and the Matterhorn Bobsleds. These lines allow individuals to fill in available seats at attractions, bypassing much of the standard queue. It's an ideal option for those who don't mind splitting up from their party during the ride itself.

Benefits of Using Single Rider Lines

- **Reduced Wait Times:** The primary advantage of using single-rider lines is the potential for significantly reduced wait times. While regular queues can take upwards of an hour or more, single-rider lines often move much faster, allowing you to take advantage of shorter wait periods.

- **Maximizing Ride Time:** For guests looking to experience as many rides as possible, single-rider lines can be an effective strategy. By decreasing the time spent in line, you can free up more of your day to explore other attractions, shows, and dining experiences within the park.

How to Use Single Rider Lines Effectively

- **Prioritize High-Demand Rides:** Use single-rider lines at attractions known for long wait times. This is particularly effective for thrill rides and newer attractions where queues tend to be longest. Prioritizing these can save you significant time.

- **Communicate with Ride Operators:** Always communicate with the ride operators when you approach the single-rider line. They can provide you with specific instructions or updates on wait times. Understanding how the process works at each ride can improve your overall experience.

- **Be Prepared to Split Up:** If you're visiting with family or friends, ensure everyone understands that using the single rider line means you'll likely be split up during the ride. Discuss this ahead of time to avoid any confusion or disappointment.

- **Combine with Other Line Strategies:** Single-rider lines can be used in conjunction with FastPass or Lightning Lane selections. Strategically plan your day by using FastPass for some must-do rides and single-rider lines for others, optimizing your overall wait times across the park.

- **Know Which Rides Offer Single Rider:** Not all rides offer a single-rider option, so it's essential to know which ones do. This information can be found on the Disneyland app or by inquiring at guest services. Planning your route around these attractions can make your visit more efficient.

Tips for a Smooth Single Rider Experience

- **Early or Late Day Use:** Consider using single rider lines during peak times, such as midday when lines are longest, or alternatively, early in the day or late in the evening when general queues may already be shorter.

- **Prepare for a Varied Experience:** Each time you use a single rider line, your experience may vary. Sometimes, you'll board almost immediately; other times, you might wait longer than expected. Remain flexible and patient.

- **Use Waiting Time Wisely:** While in any line, use your wait time to plan other parts of your day. Check the app for show times, make dining reservations, or adjust your itinerary as needed.

- **Enjoy the Solo Ride:** If you find yourself riding alone, embrace the opportunity to meet new people or simply enjoy the moment of solitude amidst a busy day.

Using single-rider lines effectively can drastically improve your Disneyland experience, allowing you to enjoy more rides with less waiting. This strategy is perfect for those who are flexible, visiting alone or with a group that doesn't mind splitting up to maximize their time at the park. By incorporating single-rider lines into your visit, you can ensure a more efficient and enjoyable adventure in Disneyland.

Engaging with Attractions When Crowds Are Thinned

Visiting Disneyland is an exhilarating experience, but navigating through massive crowds can sometimes detract from the magic. Fortunately, there are moments throughout the day when crowds thin out, presenting an ideal opportunity to engage more deeply with attractions. Understanding when these times occur and how to take advantage of them can significantly enhance your Disneyland experience.

Identifying Low Crowd Times

- **Early Morning and Late Evening:** The first few hours after the park opening and the last few hours before closing are typically the least crowded times at Disneyland. Many guests prefer to arrive mid-morning and leave after the evening fireworks or parades, so plan to start your day early or stay late to make the most of shorter lines and less crowded attractions.

- **During Parades and Shows:** Large-scale events like parades and nighttime shows tend to draw huge crowds, leaving ride lines significantly shorter. This can be a strategic time to visit popular attractions that otherwise have long wait times during normal hours.

- **Off-Peak Season Visits:** Visiting Disneyland during the off-peak season (late winter and early spring or fall) means fewer crowds overall and more frequent opportunities throughout the day when attractions are less busy.

Strategies for Engaging with Attractions

- **Take Time to Explore Details:** Disneyland's attractions are known for their attention to detail. With thinner crowds, you have a unique chance to slow down and appreciate the intricacies of each ride and themed area. For instance, explore the queue of Indiana Jones Adventure, which is filled with hidden messages and props that enhance the storyline.

- **Interactive Elements:** Many attractions include interactive elements designed to entertain guests as they wait. With fewer people, you have more time and space to engage with these features. For example, in the queue for Peter Pan's Flight, guests can interact with shadows and bells in Tinker Bell's playroom, which can be more enjoyable without the pressure of a moving line.

- **Multiple Rides:** Lower crowd levels mean you can often experience your favorite rides multiple times in succession with minimal wait. This is especially beneficial for rides like Space Mountain or Big Thunder Mountain

Railroad, where different seating positions can offer new perspectives and experiences.

- **Character Interactions:** With fewer guests around, character interactions can become more personal and extended. Characters may have more time to engage in playful antics or offer unique photo opportunities, making for memorable moments.

- **Ask Cast Members for Secrets and Tips:** Disneyland cast members are a wealth of knowledge and often willing to share interesting facts and secrets about the attractions, especially when it's less crowded, and they have more time to interact.

Making the Most of Thinned Crowds

- **Plan Around Known Quiet Times:** If you know when a parade, show or fireworks display is scheduled, plan to hit popular rides during these times. Also, consider the early morning and late evening for lower crowd levels.

- **Be Flexible:** While it's good to have a plan, being flexible allows you to take advantage of unexpected lulls in crowd levels. If you notice a sudden drop in wait times, be ready to change your plans and seize the opportunity.

- **Utilize the Disneyland App:** Continuously monitor the Disneyland app for up-to-date wait times and attraction closures. This tool is invaluable for adapting your plan on the go based on real-time information.

- **Relax and Enjoy the Atmosphere:** Fewer crowds also mean more opportunities to simply enjoy the ambiance of the park. Take a leisurely walk through Mickey's Toontown, sit by the Rivers of America, or enjoy a quiet coffee on Main Street, U.S.A., and soak in the details that make Disneyland unique.

Engaging with Disneyland attractions when crowds are thinned maximizes your time and enhances the quality of your experience. By strategically planning your visit and being prepared to adapt to the day's dynamics, you can enjoy a more relaxed, immersive visit to The Happiest Place on Earth.

Tips for Maximizing Your Day with a Well-Timed Plan

A trip to Disneyland is a magical experience, but without a well-timed plan, it's easy to feel overwhelmed by the choices and crowds. To truly maximize your day and ensure a smooth, enjoyable visit to the park, careful timing, and strategic planning are key.

Here are some essential tips to help you navigate Disneyland efficiently, ensuring that every minute of your adventure is as magical as possible.

Start with a Solid Plan

- **Research Before You Go:** Before arriving at Disneyland, familiarize yourself with the layout of the park, key attractions, and any scheduled shows or parades. Decide which attractions are must-sees for your group and check if they offer FastPass or have a reputation for long lines.

- **Prioritize Your List:** Not all attractions are created equal in terms of wait time and appeal. Prioritize rides that typically have longer wait times or are especially important to your group. Plan to hit these attractions early in the day or during typical showtimes when lines may be shorter.

- **Use the Official Disneyland App:** The Disneyland app is invaluable for real-time park information. Use it to check wait times, show schedules, character greeting times, and make dining reservations or place mobile food orders. This can save significant time and help you make decisions on the fly.

Timing Your Arrival

- **Arrive Early:** Plan to arrive at the park before it opens. Often, the first few hours after opening are the least crowded, making it an ideal time to experience the most popular attractions with minimal wait.

- **Take Advantage of Magic Hours:** If you're staying at a Disneyland Resort hotel, take advantage of Magic Hours, which allows you early entry to the parks. This can be a game-changer for accessing high-demand attractions before the general public.

Navigating the Park

- **Follow a Logical Route:** Start at the back of the park and work your way forward, or vice versa, based on your priority list. This minimizes backtracking and wasted time. Disneyland is large, and the less you crisscross, the more you'll conserve energy and time.

- **Use Single-Rider Lines:** If you don't mind splitting up your party on certain rides, use the single-rider lines, which can significantly reduce your wait time.

- **Plan Meal Times Wisely:** Avoid dining at peak lunch (11:30 AM to 1:30 PM) and dinner times (5:30 PM to 7:30 PM). Early or late meals mean you'll spend less time in line at restaurants and more time enjoying attractions while others are eating.

Adapting to the Day

- **Stay Flexible:** Even the best-laid plans may need adjustment based on crowd levels, unexpected ride closures, or just the energy levels of your group. Be ready to switch things around as needed.

- **Monitor Attraction Wait Times:** Keep an eye on the Disneyland app throughout the day for wait times. If you see a sudden drop in wait times for a priority attraction, take advantage of the moment.

Taking Breaks

- **Schedule Downtime:** Don't underestimate the need for breaks, especially if visiting with children or during the hotter months. Schedule time to rest in quieter areas of the park, like Tom Sawyer Island or the Animation Academy, or find a secluded bench in one of the less crowded lands.

- **Enjoy the Shows:** Use showtimes as an opportunity to rest and recharge. Shows like "Frozen Live at the Hyperion" or "Mickey and the Magical Map" offer entertaining breaks where you can sit, enjoy the entertainment, and rest up for more rides.

Ending Your Day

- **Stay Late:** Crowds often thin out in the evening, especially after the fireworks. Many guests leave right after the nighttime spectacular, so sticking around can give you a few extra rides with shorter wait times.

- **Last Hour Strategy:** Many attractions run up until the official park closing time. Lines for rides are closed at this time, but anyone in line before then can still ride. This last hour can be a great time to squeeze in one or two final rides.

By following these tips and planning your day with strategic timing in mind, you can ensure a fun and fruitful visit to Disneyland. You will maximize your time effectively and also create a more relaxed and enjoyable experience for everyone in your group.

Chapter 5

Enjoying Food and Drink Without the Rush

Amidst the frenetic energy of Disneyland, finding a quiet corner to savor a meal can be as rewarding as discovering a secluded cafe in a vibrant city. For those who prefer to dine away from the crowds, there are strategies and spots within the park that offer respite and relaxation, allowing one to indulge in culinary delights without the usual hustle associated with a day at Disneyland.

Selecting the Ideal Dining Time

Timing is everything when it comes to enjoying a peaceful meal at Disneyland. While most visitors queue for lunch between noon and 2 PM and dinner from 6 PM to 8 PM, choosing off-peak hours can significantly improve your dining experience. Opting for an early lunch around 11 AM or a later dinner after 8 PM can help you avoid the rush, providing a more relaxed atmosphere to enjoy your meal. Similarly, dining during popular showtimes, such as parades and nighttime spectaculars, can also mean fewer diners at restaurants.

Choosing the Right Locations

Disneyland hosts a variety of dining options that are tucked away from the main pathways and offer a quieter dining experience. For instance, the Royal Street Veranda in New Orleans Square offers a quaint spot to enjoy a quick bite, with lesser foot traffic and a view of the Rivers of America. Another hidden gem is the Hungry Bear Restaurant in Critter Country, where you can find seating on the lower deck right by the water, offering a peaceful backdrop as you dine.

Utilizing Mobile Ordering

To further streamline your dining experience and minimize time spent in queues, take advantage of Disneyland's mobile ordering service, which is available through the Disneyland app. This feature allows you to order food in advance from select restaurants and pick it up at a designated window.

Embracing the Experience

Dining in Disneyland is not just about refueling but also about enjoying the unique themes and culinary offerings each restaurant brings. Take the time to explore menus and choose places that might offer a quieter environment, such as the Blue Bayou Restaurant, which, despite its popularity, provides a serene dining experience with its indoor setting reminiscent of a night in the Louisiana Bayou. Here, the soft lighting and the gentle hum of the neighboring Pirates of the Caribbean ride create an ambiance that's both immersive and tranquil.

Section 1

Dining Options

Navigating the culinary landscape of Disneyland for those who seek solace from the crowds necessitates a blend of strategy and timing. The park offers a myriad of dining experiences, from quick bites to immersive thematic meals. Knowing where and when to dine can transform a simple meal into a peaceful retreat.

Off-the-Beaten-Path Eateries

For those looking to escape the lively crowds, certain eateries offer not just food but a quiet nook to unwind. Tucked away in corners of the park, these locations provide a reprieve from the sensory overload of more popular areas. For instance, the Harbour Galley, located in a discreet corner of Critter Country, offers a serene view of the Rivers of America. The menu here is simple and hearty, and it serves as a quick stop rather than a dining destination, making it perfect for introverts.

Similarly, the French Market Restaurant in New Orleans Square provides a shaded dining area accompanied by the soft jazz melodies that define the area. The food is a delightful mix of Southern classics, allowing for a leisurely meal away from the throes of the main thoroughfares.

Timing Your Meals

Strategically timing your meals is crucial in avoiding crowds. Dining during conventional meal times—namely lunch and dinner—often coincides with peak crowd levels. Instead, opting for an early lunch or a late dinner can ensure a more relaxed atmosphere. Many restaurants begin serving lunch as early as 11:00 AM, and by arriving shortly before this time, you can enjoy a more tranquil dining experience before the noon rush begins.

Dinner is served in most sit-down restaurants until the park closes, which presents a similar opportunity. Eating later in the evening, particularly during or just after the nighttime shows when most guests are preoccupied, affords a quieter setting.

Utilizing Mobile Ordering

To further enhance your dining experience, Disneyland's mobile ordering service allows you to bypass the conventional queueing process. Available through the Disneyland app, this service lets you order ahead from select restaurants and pick up your food at a designated window. This is particularly advantageous for those who prefer minimal interaction and wish to avoid standing in crowded lines.

Themed Dining for a Quiet Escape

For those seeking not just a meal but an experience, Disneyland offers several themed dining options that can provide a quiet escape in plain sight. The Blue Bayou Restaurant, albeit popular, offers a unique "evening" ambiance throughout the day, thanks to its indoor setting that mimics a night in the Louisiana Bayou. The restaurant's design includes secluded tables that offer a dimly lit refuge from the busy park.

In conclusion, dining at Disneyland doesn't have to be a hurried affair amidst the crowds. By choosing less frequented eateries, timing your meals strategically, utilizing mobile ordering, and selecting restaurants that offer both culinary and sensory reprieves, you can enjoy your dining experience in relative peace. These strategies allow you to recharge in the midst of a busy day exploring Disneyland, ensuring that each meal complements your trip through the happiest place on Earth.

Best Quick-Service Restaurants with Shorter Lines

In the sprawling expanse of Disneyland, where crowds swell like the tides, and the pursuit of a quick meal can often lead to daunting lines, there exist hidden culinary havens that offer respite. For those who find solace in quieter spaces, discovering the best quick-service restaurants with shorter wait times is akin to uncovering a secluded cove in a vibrant port city.

The Little-known Delights of Pacific Wharf Café

Nestled in the heart of Disney California Adventure Park, Pacific Wharf Café is a gem often overlooked by those rushing toward more flamboyant attractions. This eatery offers a variety of hearty, comforting foods, such as soups served in sourdough bread bowls, which mirror the culinary traditions of San Francisco. The setting here, inspired by a working seaside wharf, provides a backdrop that is both thematic and tranquil, where one can enjoy a meal with minimal interruption.

Bengal Barbecue: A Taste of Adventure

In the shadow of the Indiana Jones Adventure lies Bengal Barbecue, an outpost that serves as a sanctuary from the throngs of Adventureland. Known for its savory skewers of chicken, beef, and vegetables, this spot offers a quick bite without the usual wait found at other eateries in the area. The proximity to major attractions, coupled with the efficiency of its service, makes Bengal Barbecue an ideal spot for those seeking a swift and satisfying meal.

French Market Restaurant: A Touch of New Orleans

While not as quick as traditional counter-service restaurants, the French Market Restaurant in New Orleans Square provides a speedier dining experience than its table-service counterparts, with the added benefit of live jazz music that can soothe any weary traveler's soul. Offering dishes like jambalaya and Creole salad, this establishment encapsulates the vibrancy of New Orleans dining without the usual bustle, making it a favorite for those in search of flavor and peace in equal measure.

Refreshment Corner: Hot Dogs with a Side of History

On the corner of Main Street, U.S.A., the Refreshment Corner, sponsored by Coca-Cola, offers more than just quick bites—it offers a slice of Americana that is often passed by as guests hurry towards the castle. The menu is simple, featuring classic hot dogs and pretzels, but the real allure is the nostalgic setting, complete with ragtime piano melodies that play tunes from yesteryears, inviting one to linger over a meal longer than they might elsewhere.

Flo's V8 Café: A Route 66 Retreat

In Cars Land, Flo's V8 Café stands out not just for its clever automotive-themed décor but also for its often shorter lines compared to other dining options in Disney California Adventure. The menu, which features American diner classics such as burgers and fries, is perfectly aligned with the thematic Route 66 experience. The indoor seating provides a panoramic view of the Radiator Springs Racers, offering both comfort and entertainment as you dine.

Tips for Enjoying These Spaces

- **Visit During Off-Peak Hours:** Even at these lesser-known spots, timing is crucial. Aim for late morning or mid-afternoon meals to avoid the typical lunch and dinner rushes.

- **Utilize Mobile Ordering:** Where available, use Disneyland's mobile ordering service to minimize waiting times even further. This allows you to order from anywhere in the park and pick up your food when it's ready.

- **Combine Dining with Rest:** Each of these locations offers unique seating areas where one can take a moment to relax. Plan your meal times around your need for a break, enjoying the dual benefits of nourishment and rest.

In Disneyland, where every moment is precious, knowing where to dine without the wait can significantly enhance your experience. These quick-service restaurants offer not just a meal but a pleasant pause in your tour, allowing you to savor both the food and the moment away from the crowds.

Finding Hidden Snack Spots Throughout the Park

In the vibrant expanse of Disneyland, amid the echoing laughter and the distant music of parades, there lies a challenge for those who cherish solitude and seek to escape the relentless crowds. Like a traveler exploring a well-trodden city and finding solace in its less-known streets, the introverted visitor to Disneyland can discover hidden snack spots that offer a peaceful respite from the chaos. These hidden gems provide unique culinary delights and a moment of quiet in the midst of a busy day.

The Secret of Bengal Barbecue

Tucked away in Adventureland, Bengal Barbecue is often overshadowed by its more flamboyant neighbors. This small but mighty snack station offers a variety of exotic grilled skewers, from spicy beef to sweet pineapple. The proximity to the Indiana Jones Adventure and the Jungle Cruise makes it an ideal stop for a quick bite, yet its counter-service setup means shorter lines and quicker service, allowing one to enjoy a savory treat amidst a shaded, less crowded area.

Al Fresco Tasting Terrace

For those in the know, the Al Fresco Tasting Terrace, accessible only to those with Legacy Passholder access, provides an exclusive escape atop the Golden Vine Winery building in California Adventure. This hidden spot is not just a place for exquisite wine and appetizers but also offers a panoramic view of the park, creating a serene backdrop to enjoy select Californian wines and Mediterranean-inspired small plates. It's a perfect enclave for those seeking a quiet moment away from the lively paths below.

The Quiet Charm of Maurice's Treats

Near the Fantasy Faire, a medieval-themed area designed for meeting Disney princesses lies Maurice's Treats. This modest snack cart is a treasure trove of delightful twists on traditional snacks, offering chocolate-dipped pretzels and a unique strawberry twist. The area around Maurice's Treats is often less crowded, offering benches and shaded spots where one can enjoy a snack while indulging in the quieter side of the park's festive atmosphere.

Refreshment Corner at Cozy Cone Motel

In Cars Land, the Cozy Cone Motel offers a clever take on the classic American road trip experience with its cone-themed snack kiosks. Each cone serves a different treat, from churros and ice cream to savory bites like chili con queso. The layout encourages wandering from cone to cone, and the clever seating inside oversized traffic cones provides a whimsical yet secluded spot to enjoy a quick snack. The playful theme and attention to detail in the décor make it an enjoyable retreat.

Hidden Oasis at Tropical Hideaway

Nestled near the Enchanted Tiki Room, Tropical Hideaway is one of the newer additions to Disneyland's dining options and offers a secluded paradise for those in search of exotic flavors. This marketplace serves up a tantalizing array of tropical snacks, including bao buns, sweet pineapple lumpia, and Dole Whip. The seating area, overlooking the Jungle Cruise River, provides a hidden oasis where one can relax and savor the flavors in relative peace.

Tips for Enjoying Hidden Snack Spots

- **Plan Visits During Off-Peak Hours:** Even hidden spots can attract crowds during peak meal times. Plan to visit these snack locations during off-peak hours, such as late morning or mid-afternoon, to avoid the larger crowds.

- **Use Mobile Ordering Where Available:** Take advantage of Disneyland's mobile ordering system to minimize waiting time and maximize convenience.

- **Combine Snacking with People-Watching:** Many of these hidden spots provide excellent opportunities for people-watching, adding another layer of enjoyment to your quiet snack break.

By seeking out these less conspicuous snack spots, the introverted traveler can enjoy the culinary delights of Disneyland without being overwhelmed by crowded eateries.

Each hidden snack spot offers unique treats and an invitation to pause and refresh, much like a quiet station stop on a long railway trip, providing a moment of calm before the next adventure.

Tips for Enjoying Character Dining Experiences Without the Chaos

Character dining at Disneyland is a quintessential part of the magical experience, offering memorable interactions with beloved Disney characters while enjoying a hearty meal. However, for those who prefer less crowded environments, these joyful encounters can sometimes feel overwhelming. By adopting a thoughtful approach reminiscent of a seasoned traveler who navigates busy marketplaces yet finds quiet corners for contemplation, you can enjoy these enchanting experiences without the usual hustle and bustle.

Choose the Right Venue and Time

- **Selecting the Right Restaurant:** Disneyland offers several character dining options, each with its own atmosphere and character lineup. For a more subdued experience, consider dining at venues known for being less hectic. For example, Storytellers Café at Disney's Grand Californian Hotel offers a rustic setting with occasional visits from Disney characters in a less crowded environment compared to the busy Goofy's Kitchen.

- **Timing Your Reservation:** Timing is crucial in avoiding large crowds. Booking an early breakfast or a late lunch can help you miss the peak dining times, which typically see higher volumes of guests. These off-peak hours provide a more relaxed atmosphere, allowing for more personal interactions with the characters.

Utilize Advance Reservations

- **Booking Early:** Disneyland allows reservations for character dining up to 60 days in advance. Securing your reservation early ensures your spot and gives you the advantage of choosing the best times that align with quieter dining periods. This foresight is akin to planning travel routes in less-trodden paths, providing a smoother and more enjoyable tour.

Prepare for the Experience

- **Setting Expectations:** If traveling with children or guests unfamiliar with character dining, prepare them for what to expect. Discussing the characters that may visit the table and the general flow of the meal can help manage excitement levels and make the experience more enjoyable for everyone involved.

- **Arriving Prepared:** Arriving a few minutes early for your reservation can also significantly enhance your experience. Use this time to settle into the space, familiarize yourself with the setting, and relax before the characters begin making their rounds.

Engage Thoughtfully with Characters

- **Interaction Tips:** When characters visit your table, engage with them as you would in a quieter, one-on-one meeting. Have your autograph book ready, think of questions you might ask, and prepare your camera for quick photos. This preparation allows you to make the most of the time with each character without feeling rushed.

- **Enjoy the Moment:** Just as a traveler might savor a quiet moment in a vibrant city, take the time to enjoy the interactions. The characters are skilled at engaging guests of all ages, making each visit unique. Appreciate the nuances of their costumes, the context of their stories, and the joy they bring to diners.

Choose Less Popular Characters

- **Opt for Unique Characters:** Some character dining experiences feature less mainstream characters who might not attract as large of a crowd as the classic Disney princesses or Mickey Mouse. Dining experiences like the breakfast at Plaza Inn, featuring lesser-known characters, can offer more relaxed encounters.

Follow Up with Appreciation

- **Showing Gratitude:** Just as a seasoned traveler appreciates the hidden gems found along the way, show appreciation for the staff and characters who make these dining experiences memorable. A simple thank you can make the interaction more personal and rewarding.

By integrating these strategies into your character dining experience at Disneyland, you can transform what is often a chaotic meal into a delightful encounter. These meals can become cherished memories reminiscent of quiet interludes in a trek filled with discovery and wonder.

Section 2

Relaxing Locations for Meals

For those seeking refuge from the lively pathways and eager throngs of Disneyland, serene oases exist that offer nourishment both for the body and the soul. Finding a tranquil spot for a meal amidst the excitement can transform a day at the park, turning a simple dining break into a moment of respite and rejuvenation.

The Blue Bayou: Dining in the Heart of Adventure

Nestled inside the Pirates of the Caribbean attraction, The Blue Bayou Restaurant presents one of the most unique dining experiences Disneyland has to offer. Here, patrons can enjoy Cajun and Creole cuisine while seated at candlelit tables that line the shores of the attraction's indoor bayou. The perpetual twilight setting, combined with the soft chirping of crickets and the distant songs of pirates, creates a tranquil backdrop that feels worlds apart from the park outside. This restaurant's location is not just a place to eat but a retreat where one can linger over a meal and feel transported to a serene, Southern evening.

Alfresco Tasting Terrace: A Hidden Gem

Exclusively accessible to Legacy Passholders and hidden atop the Golden Vine Winery in Disney California Adventure, the Alfresco Tasting Terrace offers a secluded getaway. This spot specializes in serving up California-inspired appetizers and a selection of wines from vineyards that have ties to Disney's history. The terrace overlooks Radiator Springs and provides a quiet, shaded area to enjoy a glass of wine and a light snack away from the crowds below. The ambiance here is reminiscent of a private vineyard visit, making it an ideal spot for those in search of peace and a touch of elegance.

Hungry Bear Restaurant: Riverside Repose

At the edge of Critter Country, the Hungry Bear Restaurant offers a more laid-back dining experience with its expansive views of the Rivers of America. This counter-service restaurant serves classic American fare and features ample outdoor seating on two levels. The lower deck, in particular, is often less crowded and provides a peaceful setting where guests can watch the Mark Twain Riverboat glide by. The natural scenery and the distant sounds of the water make this location perfect for those looking to unwind and enjoy a slower pace during their park visit.

Relaxation and Reflection at Red Rose Taverne

Located in Fantasyland, the Red Rose Taverne is a charming eatery themed after "Beauty and the Beast." While it can be crowded at times, its interior offers a cozy, cottage-like atmosphere where visitors can enjoy French-inspired dishes. The detailed decor, from stained glass windows to portraits of characters, offers diners visual treats that complement the culinary ones. Choosing to dine during off-peak hours here can result in a quiet, contemplative meal amidst the enchantment of a beloved fairy tale.

These dining locations within Disneyland and Disney California Adventure offer excellent food and provide environments conducive to relaxation and reflection. Choosing to dine at these specially selected spots allows guests who prefer solitude to step away from the sensory overload of the parks and enjoy a moment of quiet amid the magic of Disney.

Where to Find Outdoor Seating with a View

In the vibrant mosaic of Disneyland, where each turn offers a spectacle, and every alley holds a story, finding a quiet corner with a scenic view can provide a much-needed respite for those who treasure solitude amidst the excitement. Outdoor seating that offers both comfort and a picturesque vista can transform a simple break into a refreshing retreat, allowing one to absorb the wonder of Disneyland at a leisurely pace.

The Charm of New Orleans Square

For those seeking an immersive atmosphere coupled with a visual treat, the balconies and terraces of New Orleans Square offer a prime locale. One of the best spots in this area is the balcony seating at Café Orleans. Here, guests can enjoy classic dishes like the Monte Cristo sandwich while overlooking the lively streets below, which are filled with the sounds of jazz and the sight of passersby meandering through the quaint market-style pathways. The riverfront area also provides a serene view of the Rivers of America, where the occasional sight of the Mark Twain Riverboat adds to the charm of dining in this historic district.

Tranquility at the Pacific Wharf

The Pacific Wharf in Disney California Adventure offers a different pace and ambiance. This area, inspired by San Francisco's waterfront, features a variety of dining options with ample outdoor seating. The wharf's layout encourages wandering and discovering hidden nooks where one can sit and enjoy the waterfront views. A notable spot is the Mendocino Terrace at the Golden Vine Winery, where guests can savor a glass of wine alongside views of the scenic vineyard-themed backdrop, providing a quiet escape from the more crowded parts of the park.

Alpine Views at Edelweiss Snacks

Tucked away beside the Matterhorn Bobsleds, Edelweiss Snacks offers a quaint outdoor seating area that looks out over the crystal waters of the submarine lagoon and the towering peak of the Matterhorn. This lesser-known spot serves up simple fare such as turkey legs and corn on the cob, which can be enjoyed at picnic tables that offer a secluded spot away from the main thoroughfares. The backdrop of the Swiss mountain and the soothing sounds of the nearby water make this a refreshing stop.

Lakeside Dining at Hungry Bear Restaurant

Further seclusion can be found at the Hungry Bear Restaurant in Critter Country, where the lower decks provide a peaceful dining experience on the banks of the Rivers of America. This location is often quieter and offers a direct view of the river traffic and the lush greenery across the water. The gentle flow of the river and the shaded tables make it an ideal spot for those wishing to take a longer break, enjoying both the food and the tranquil surroundings.

Grand Vistas at Lamplight Lounge

For a panoramic view that captures the essence of Disney California Adventure, the Lamplight Lounge on Pixar Pier offers expansive outdoor seating that overlooks the busy boardwalk below. The lounge's elevated position provides a sweeping view of the pier and the glistening Paradise Bay. With a menu that features creative, Pixar-inspired cuisine and cocktails, the Lamplight Lounge is a perfect spot for those looking to blend a gourmet experience with striking views.

Each of these locations within Disneyland and Disney California Adventure provides not just a meal but a moment of peace. Outdoor seating with a view allows visitors to take in the sights and sounds of the park from a comfortable distance, offering a visual feast that complements the culinary one. For those who find joy in quieter observations, these spots offer a welcome pause, a breath of fresh air amidst the whirlwind of Disney magic.

The Charm of Napa Rose and Its Quieter Atmosphere

Nestled within the grand confines of Disney's Grand Californian Hotel & Spa, Napa Rose stands as a beacon of culinary excellence and serene dining. This esteemed restaurant, known for its sophisticated ambiance and exemplary service, offers a refuge from the vibrant energy of Disneyland parks, presenting a perfect dining haven for those seeking quiet alongside a fine dining experience.

A Sanctuary of Culinary Delight

Napa Rose's design and architecture draw heavily on the influences of California's renowned Napa Valley, integrating wood and stone elements that echo the region's rustic elegance. The restaurant's expansive windows overlook lush landscapes, offering diners tranquil views that complement the serene atmosphere. This setting is not merely a backdrop but an integral part of the dining experience, inviting guests to relax and engage with the space as they would with a scenic vista during a tranquil train trip through the countryside.

Exquisite Cuisine with a View

Under the guidance of Executive Chef Andrew Sutton, Napa Rose offers a menu that celebrates the bounty of California with ingredients sourced from local farms and fisheries. The seasonal menu ensures that each visit can offer a new culinary exploration, much like the ever-changing landscapes viewed from a train window. Diners can indulge in dishes that are both innovative and comforting, from expertly prepared seafood to hearty, farm-fresh produce that showcases the richness of the region's cuisine.

An Intimate Dining Experience

What sets Napa Rose apart, particularly for those who prefer a quieter dining atmosphere, is its commitment to providing an intimate experience. The restaurant features a variety of seating options that cater to different desires for privacy and comfort. The main dining area, with its well-spaced tables and soft lighting, is perfect for those who enjoy a gentle hum of distant conversations. For a more secluded setting, the chef's counter offers an interactive experience where diners can observe the artistry of the kitchen while enjoying personalized attention from the chefs.

The Vintner's Table: A Unique Culinary Tour

For guests looking for an exclusive and quiet dining experience, Napa Rose offers the Vintner's Table—a weekly event where Chef Sutton curates a special four-course menu paired with exceptional wines. This experience provides a feast for the senses and an opportunity to engage with the chef's culinary vision in a more personal setting. The Vintner's Table is held in a private part of the restaurant, ensuring a secluded environment that appeals to those seeking solitude and a slower dining pace.

Reservations and Planning

Securing a reservation at Napa Rose is essential, particularly if one aims to capture a specific atmosphere, such as a quiet corner or a seat at the chef's counter. Reservations can be made up to 60 days in advance, allowing ample time for planning and ensuring availability. For those visiting Disneyland seeking a reprieve from the day's excitement, timing a dinner at Napa Rose towards the evening can serve as a perfect conclusion to a day of adventure, transitioning into a night of relaxation and gourmet satisfaction.

Exploring Nearby Off-Site Restaurants for a Break from the Park

For those who treasure quiet moments and seek to escape the vibrant chaos of Disneyland, the surrounding area offers a selection of off-site restaurants that provide a culinary respite and a momentary retreat from the sensory overload of the park.

Quiet Culinary Havens in Anaheim

Anaheim, the city that hosts Disneyland, is rich with dining venues that cater to every taste and provide environments far removed from the thematic intensity of the park.

- **The Ranch Restaurant & Saloon**

Just a short drive from Disneyland, The Ranch Restaurant & Saloon offers a serene dining experience with a focus on superb farm-to-table cuisine. The restaurant prides itself on serving dishes crafted from locally sourced ingredients, with a menu that highlights the best of American regional cuisine. The atmosphere here is refined and tranquil, ideal for those who appreciate a quieter dining environment.

- **Habana**

Located in the nearby LAB Anti-Mall, Habana offers a taste of Cuba in the heart of Southern California. This restaurant provides a lush, tropical ambiance that feels worlds apart from the nearby Disney attractions. Guests can enjoy authentic Cuban dishes while relaxing in a beautifully decorated setting that features indoor and outdoor seating surrounded by greenery and soft lighting.

- **Anaheim Packing District**

For those who enjoy a variety of options, the Anaheim Packing District presents a unique opportunity. This culinary hub, housed in a renovated 1919 citrus-packing house, features an assortment of eateries ranging from modern American to international street foods. The layout of the district encourages leisurely exploration, with communal seating areas that provide a relaxed atmosphere away from the hustle of Disneyland.

Enjoying a Seaside Meal

Watertable at the Hyatt Regency Huntington Beach

A slightly longer excursion from Disneyland can take visitors to the Watertable at the Hyatt Regency Huntington Beach. This fine-dining restaurant offers sophisticated American fare with a focus on seasonal ingredients. The added allure is its location—overlooking the Pacific Ocean, providing diners with soothing seaside views and a calming atmosphere that complements the exquisite meals.

A Little Italy in Anaheim

Brunos Italian Kitchen

Just a few minutes from Disneyland, Brunos Italian Kitchen offers a cozy retreat with its warm, inviting atmosphere and hearty Italian cuisine. The restaurant focuses on delivering classic Italian dishes in a setting that encourages diners to linger over their meals, enjoying a glass of wine and engaging in conversations away from the park's frenzy.

Planning Your Dining Escape

To fully enjoy these off-site dining experiences, planning is key:

- **Reservations are recommended**, especially for dinner. Many restaurants can be fully booked days in advance, so securing a spot early ensures you won't have to wait.

- **Consider transportation options.** While some restaurants may be within walking distance, others might require a short drive or a ride in a taxi or rideshare service.

- **Time your visit for a midday or evening meal.** This allows you to break up your day at Disneyland or conclude your visit with a relaxing dinner.

Exploring nearby off-site restaurants offers more than just a meal—it provides a pause in your Disneyland adventure, a chance to recharge in a setting that contrasts with the energy of the theme park.

Chapter 6

Embracing the Disneyland Experience

For an introverted traveler, Disneyland might initially seem like a realm tailored exclusively for the extroverted and the endlessly energetic. Yet beneath its vibrant surface lies a layered experience, rich with quiet corners and contemplative moments that allow even the most reserved visitors to embrace the magic on their own terms. By navigating the park with a thoughtful strategy, introverts can uncover a different kind of Disneyland adventure—one that balances the joyous cacophony with moments of peaceful solitude.

Finding Solitude Amidst Celebration

Disneyland is renowned not just for its rides but for the immersive experiences it offers. For those who revel in observation more than participation, the park presents numerous opportunities to engage quietly. One can find solace in the meticulous landscaping of the less-trafficked paths, like the gardens near the Royal Theatre, or in the intricate architectural details found in the queues of attractions like the Indiana Jones Adventure. These details often go unnoticed by the typical hurried guest but can offer deep appreciation for introverts who thrive on the subtler aspects of their surroundings.

Strategic Ride Timing

Choosing when to explore popular attractions can significantly enhance the introvert's experience. Riding the Disneyland Railroad for a full loop offers not just a respite from walking but also a chance to absorb the park's layout and enjoy its sights without the crowd's pressure. Similarly, timing a visit to major attractions during parades or nighttime shows when most guests are otherwise occupied can reduce the stress of long lines and crowded spaces.

Appreciating Themed Dining Exclusively

Dining at Disneyland doesn't have to be a rushed affair amidst noisy cafeterias. Restaurants like the Blue Bayou offer a quieter, more immersive dining experience with views of passing boats from Pirates of the Caribbean, encapsulating a perfect blend of culinary delight and visual splendor in a less frenetic setting. Booking an off-time meal here can provide a serene pause in your day, allowing for a leisurely meal that also serves as a recharge for the adventures that lie ahead.

Participating in Scheduled Events

For introverts, scheduled events such as guided tours or nighttime spectaculars provide structured experiences that allow for enjoyment within a set framework. Participating in a guided tour, for example, can provide insights and stories about the park that deepen one's appreciation and connection to the environment, all while navigating the space in a small, manageable group.

Embrace the Night

As the day winds down, many areas of Disneyland take on a new persona that favors the introvert. The crowds thin, the lights dim, and the atmosphere shifts to a more relaxed vibe. Attractions like Tomorrowland at night offer a visually stunning experience with fewer people and a more laid-back feel. It's during these times that one can fully appreciate the magic of Disneyland's evenings, from the soft glow of the lanterns in Adventureland to the spectacular fireworks display over Sleeping Beauty Castle.

In embracing Disneyland, introverts don't have to forsake their natural inclinations for quiet and introspection. Instead, they can find within the park's expanse a series of moments and experiences that resonate with their quieter, more reflective nature. With careful planning and an understanding of when and where to find these quieter moments, Disneyland opens up as a place where every visitor, regardless of temperament, can find joy and enchantment.

Section 1

Finding Your Own Pace

Exploring Disneyland, a place of boundless joy and heavy crowds, can seem daunting for those who cherish a slower, more measured approach to travel. Yet, within this lively world, there exists the opportunity to discover the park at your own pace, finding joy in its quieter corners and delight in its less-trodden paths.

Embrace Early Mornings

The early morning hours at Disneyland are a precious gift for an introverted traveler. As the gates open and the sun rises over the iconic Sleeping Beauty Castle, the park reveals itself in a more subdued light. This is when you can enjoy Main Street, U.S.A., without the usual hustle, watch the park wake up, and experience popular attractions like Peter Pan's Flight or Space Mountain before the lines lengthen. Early mornings allow you to beat the crowds and witness the park's detailed theming and landscaping in a calm, uncluttered environment.

Mid-Day Retreats

Knowing where to find tranquility becomes essential as the day progresses and the crowds swell. Disneyland is designed with numerous quiet spaces that escape the midday rush. The lesser-known pathways around the Rivers of America offer peaceful views and benches where you can sit and regroup. Similarly, the Animation Building in Disney California Adventure provides a dark, cool space to relax and immerse yourself in Disney and Pixar sketches and animations, offering a quiet respite from the external chaos.

Utilizing Technology

Leveraging the Disneyland app to plan your day can significantly enhance your experience by minimizing unnecessary waiting and walking. The app provides real-time updates on wait times, parade schedules, and showtimes, enabling you to strategize your movements around the park. For instance, if you notice a sudden drop in wait times at a usually busy ride, you can seize the opportunity to enjoy it without the usual delay.

Late Evening Exploration

As the evening sets in, Disneyland transforms into a lit spectacle, and many guests begin to depart, especially after the fireworks show. This time allows for a more leisurely exploration of the attractions. The night hours often bring shorter lines and cooler temperatures, making it ideal for enjoying outdoor rides like Big Thunder Mountain Railroad or strolling through the beautifully illuminated Sleeping Beauty Castle.

Customizing Your Experience

Remember, your visit to Disneyland is yours to design. If large crowds and noise overwhelm you, consider focusing your visit on shows and attractions off the beaten path. Rides like the Disneyland Railroad offer a complete loop around the park, providing a relaxing way to see all the lands without the fatigue of walking through crowded pathways.

Strategies for Balancing Rides and Downtime

Navigating Disneyland, a world of enchantment and excitement, calls for a delicate balance between the thrill of rides and the necessity of downtime. For many, particularly those who find solace in quieter moments, crafting a visit that includes vibrant attractions and rest periods can transform a potentially overwhelming day into an enjoyable and sustainable experience.

Prioritizing Attractions

Start your day with a clear plan by prioritizing which rides are must-sees and identifying which ones can be skipped. This decision should hinge not just on personal preference but also on understanding the layout and peak times of the park. Attractions like Space Mountain and the Indiana Jones Adventure typically see longer lines, making them ideal candidates for early morning visits or during parade times when most guests are distracted. Apps and current park guides can provide real-time data to help make these decisions more informed and strategic.

Timing Your Visits

The early morning hours immediately after the park opens are often the least crowded. This window provides an opportunity to enjoy popular rides with shorter wait times. Conversely, planning ride times during parades and fireworks—when most guests are otherwise occupied—can also result in less crowded ride experiences. For introverts or those who dislike crowds, these strategic timings can mean enjoying more rides without the stress of long lines.

Integrating Downtime

Downtime is essential, especially in a sensory-rich environment like Disneyland. Integrating breaks into your day is crucial for maintaining energy and enthusiasm. Quiet spots like the shaded areas near the Mark Twain Riverboat or the less frequented paths of Tom Sawyer Island offer peaceful retreats. Additionally, consider timing a sit-down meal during peak ride times, which offers a break and avoids the rush at restaurants.

Using Rider Switch and Single Rider Lines

For those traveling with a group with varying interests and stamina levels, utilize the Rider Switch program, which allows guests with small children to take turns riding while the others watch the child. This can minimize wait times and manage energy levels for both parents and children. Similarly, Single Rider lines available at select attractions can dramatically reduce wait times and are worth considering for those who do not mind splitting up from their party momentarily.

Planning for the Unexpected

Flexibility is key in any travel plan, especially in a dynamic environment like Disneyland. While it's important to have a plan, it's equally crucial to adapt to the day's realities—whether it's unexpected ride closures, changes in weather, or personal energy dips. Listening to your body and permitting yourself to stray from the plan for rest at the hotel or a quiet coffee break can make the difference between a good and a great visit.

Leveraging Technology

Maximize using Disneyland's mobile app not just for planning ride times but also for finding quiet moments. The app can guide you to less crowded attractions, show waiting times, and even help you order food from quieter venues, reducing the need to stand in long lines.

Embracing the Night

As the evening sets in and many families with young children start to leave, the park transforms into a more adult-friendly environment. This time can be ideal for enjoying rides with typically longer wait times during the day. The cooler temperature and lit-up ambiance also make the evening a magical experience, offering a different perspective of the park that can be more aligned with adult preferences.

How to Enjoy Live Entertainment Without Feeling Overwhelmed

For those who prefer the quieter moments, navigating the lively energy of Disneyland's live entertainment might seem daunting. Yet, with thoughtful planning and strategic approaches, even the most crowd-averse can enjoy the vibrant shows and character performances integral to the Disneyland experience.

Choosing the Right Shows

Disneyland offers a variety of live entertainment options, from grandiose nighttime spectaculars to smaller, more intimate performances. Opting for daytime shows or those in less popular venues can be a wise choice for those seeking to avoid large crowds. Shows like "The Royal Theatre" in Fantasyland present classic tales in a humorous, interactive format with a smaller audience size, providing a delightful experience without the overwhelming crowds at more prominent attractions like "Fantasmic!"

Timing is Key

When experiencing live shows, timing can significantly impact crowd levels. Attending performances during off-peak times, such as weekday afternoons or other major attractions (like the evening fireworks), can result in smaller audiences and a more relaxed viewing experience. Checking the show schedules and planning to arrive at least 15-20 minutes early can also help secure a comfortable viewing spot without needing to navigate through dense crowds.

Utilizing Alternative Viewing Areas

For major spectacles such as the "Fireworks over Sleeping Beauty's Castle," consider watching from less conventional spots where the crowds are thinner, but the view remains unobstructed. Areas around the edges of Main Street, U.S.A., or even some spots in Frontierland and near It's a Small World offer decent views without the packed feeling of the central hub. Bringing a small, portable seat or finding a place near a bench can make the wait more comfortable and the experience more enjoyable.

Taking Advantage of Dining Packages

Several dining options in Disneyland offer packages that include reserved seating for shows. Booking these can alleviate the stress of finding a good spot amidst a sea of people. Restaurants like the Blue Bayou and River Belle Terrace offer meal packages with reserved seating for shows like "Fantasmic!" This guarantees a great view and allows you to enjoy the show from a quieter, seated area, away from the standing crowds.

Embracing Smaller Acts

Beyond the major shows, Disneyland is teeming with smaller performances throughout the park. Bands in New Orleans Square, the Dapper Dans on Main Street, U.S.A., and even roaming character interactions in Fantasyland provide entertainment that can be enjoyed casually without requiring attendees to be in the thick of large groups. These performances offer the ambiance and joy of live entertainment while allowing you to control how close you get to the action.

Personal Comfort Measures

Bringing along items that can enhance personal comfort, such as noise-canceling headphones or a personal fan, can make a big difference in how you experience larger shows. These items can help mitigate sensory overload and allow you to focus on enjoying the performance itself. Additionally, knowing the locations of quieter, less crowded restrooms or rest areas nearby can provide a quick escape if a break is needed.

Reflecting on the Experience

After enjoying a live show, taking time to retreat to a quieter part of the park to reflect can be a soothing way to process and appreciate the experience. This can be especially rewarding after evening shows when parts of the park begin to quiet down as guests start to leave.

By employing these strategies, even the most introverted or crowd-sensitive visitors can successfully enjoy the live entertainment at Disneyland. The key lies in thoughtful planning, leveraging lesser-known options, and always making space for personal comfort, ensuring that every aspect of the Disneyland experience is enjoyable, not overwhelming.

Engaging with the Park's Ambiance in a Way That Feels Comfortable

For many, the allure of Disneyland is not just the thrill of its rides but the immersive ambiance that pervades the park. Yet, for those who are crowd-averse or prefer a more subdued experience, finding comfort in this busy environment requires a thoughtful approach to engaging with the park's rich atmosphere.

Early Morning Walks for Serene Exploration

One of the most effective ways to enjoy Disneyland's ambiance comfortably is by starting your day at the park early. The early hours offer a unique opportunity to experience the magic of Disneyland before the crowds swell. This is the perfect time to appreciate the meticulous attention to detail in the park's design—from the charming streets of Main Street, U.S.A., to the whimsical fantasy of Sleeping Beauty's Castle. An early morning walk through these areas allows for a serene exploration, where one can absorb the sights, sounds, and subtle beauties without the overwhelming presence of large crowds.

Discovering Quiet Corners and Hidden Gems

Even at peak times, there are pockets within Disneyland that remain relatively tranquil. These lesser-known areas can offer a peaceful refuge as well as a chance to enjoy the park's ambiance. For instance, the pathways around Tom Sawyer's Island or the quiet nooks near the Royal Theatre provide a break from the hustle and bustle, where one can sit and relax or simply enjoy people-watching. Another hidden gem is the Animation Building in California Adventure, which offers a darker, cooler environment that is often less crowded, allowing for a quiet, immersive engagement with Disney's animated classics.

Scheduled Breaks at Themed Restaurants

Incorporating scheduled breaks into your visit by planning meals at themed restaurants can also enhance your experience of the park's ambiance. Dining at places like the Blue Bayou, where you can enjoy a meal while boats glide silently by on the Pirates of the Caribbean ride, offers a unique sensory experience that is both relaxing and engaging. These meals provide a culinary break and a chance to soak in the themed environments without the strain of standing or moving through crowds.

Utilizing Special Viewing Areas for Parades and Shows

For those who wish to experience Disneyland's famous parades and nighttime shows without crowds, utilizing special viewing areas can be particularly beneficial. Many themed restaurants and reserved areas offer less crowded options for enjoying these events. Booking a dining package that includes reserved seating for shows like Fantasmic! or securing a spot in less crowded areas, such as near the It's a Small World attraction, can provide a comfortable viewing experience away from the main throngs.

Personalizing Your Interaction with Attractions

Tailoring your interaction with attractions to times when they are less crowded can also make your experience more comfortable. Using rider switch options, single rider lines or FastPass selections strategically can help manage how much you engage with the crowds at popular rides. Additionally, visiting some attractions during shows or dining hours can result in shorter lines and a more relaxed experience.

Embracing the Nighttime Magic

As the evening sets in, the park transforms with lights and shadows, creating a magical nighttime ambiance that is different from the daytime vibe. Many visitors find the nighttime enchanting and less overwhelming. Attractions like the Main

Street Electrical Parade or the quiet ambiance of Adventureland at night offer a new perspective and a more subdued experience, allowing for comfortable engagement with the park's environment.

Section 2

Mindful Travel Practices

Traveling mindfully through Disneyland, a place where sensory overload is often part of the package, can transform a potentially overwhelming visit into an enriching personal tour. For those who prefer the paths less trodden or quieter moments amidst the revelry, adopting mindful travel practices is key to embracing the full Disneyland experience while maintaining one's peace and personal space.

Planning and Preparation

Advance Planning: Mindfulness begins with preparation. Before setting foot in the park, outline your visit based on your personal preferences and tolerance levels for crowds. Utilize resources like the Disneyland app to plan your route around the park, pinpointing quieter attractions and dining options that provide a respite from the masses. Consider the timing of your visit, aiming for weekdays during the off-season when the crowds are thinner.

Setting Intentions: Start your day by setting intentions. Decide what you want to achieve from your visit, whether it's experiencing a particular ride, enjoying the landscapes, or simply observing the parade of diverse visitors. This focus will help you navigate the park purposefully and avoid aimless wandering, which can often lead to fatigue and sensory overload.

Engaging Mindfully with Attractions

Selective Queuing: Choose attractions that are known for their immersive experiences and less about the thrills, which typically attract smaller crowds. Attractions like the Enchanted Tiki Room or the Disneyland Railroad offer a chance to sit, relax, and enjoy at a slower pace. For more popular rides, use the FastPass system to minimize waiting times.

Appreciating the Details: Disneyland is renowned for its attention to detail. Take the time to appreciate the craftsmanship and creativity that go into each attraction, shop, and restaurant. This can make even a simple stroll through the park a more engaging experience. Notice the thematic elements, listen to the background music, and enjoy the landscaping — each element is carefully designed to enhance the visitor's experience.

Taking Time to Reflect

Scheduled Breaks: Mindfulness isn't just about constant movement; it's equally about pauses. Schedule breaks throughout your day at designated quiet spots around the park. Places like the benches near the Snow White Grotto or the gardens around the Royal Theatre offer peaceful settings where you can sit back and absorb the atmosphere without pressure.

Mindful Eating: Choose dining options that allow you to escape the busiest parts of the park during peak times. Opt for restaurants with outdoor seating like the Plaza Inn's patio, where you can enjoy a meal away from the main thoroughfares while people-watching and perhaps journaling about your day.

Practicing Presence

Stay Present: With so much to see and do, it's easy to focus solely on what's next and miss the magic of the moment. Practice staying present by focusing on your senses — what you see, hear, smell, and feel as you navigate the park. This can deepen your connection to the environment and enhance your overall experience.

Digital Detox: Consider limiting your use of digital devices throughout the day. While it's helpful to use the park's app for navigating and planning, constant connectivity can detract from the experience. Allow yourself time to simply enjoy being in the park, free from digital distractions.

By incorporating these mindful travel practices, your visit to Disneyland can become more than just an escape from everyday life — it can be a trip of discovery filled with meaningful moments and personal reflections. This approach enriches your experience and ensures that you engage with Disneyland in a way that respects your individual needs and preferences.

Techniques for Managing Energy Levels Throughout the Day

Navigating Disneyland, with its vast expanse and ceaseless energy, requires more than just enthusiasm; it demands careful management of one's physical and mental stamina. For those who prefer to experience the park's magic without the exhaustion that often accompanies a day of relentless fun, certain techniques can be employed to maintain energy levels, ensuring a day that is both enjoyable and sustainable.

Start with a Solid Foundation

- **A Nourishing Breakfast:** Begin your day with a balanced breakfast, whether at your hotel or at one of the park's quieter restaurants. Options like the Carnation Café on Main Street, U.S.A., offer a sit-down experience with hearty meal options that can provide sustained energy. A nutritious start fuels the body and sets a calm tone, allowing you to face the lively environment with poise.

- **Hydration is Key:** Regular hydration is crucial, especially with the amount of walking involved in exploring Disneyland. Carry a refillable water bottle and take advantage of the numerous water stations located throughout the park. Staying hydrated prevents fatigue and keeps you alert, enhancing your ability to enjoy the park's offerings.

Plan Strategic Breaks

- **Scheduled Resting Points:** Just as a seasoned traveler might plan stops along a ride, strategically scheduling breaks throughout your Disneyland visit can help in managing energy. Utilize quieter areas such as the shaded seating around the Fantasyland Theatre or the benches in less trafficked paths near the Pixie Hollow. These breaks are vital for mental and physical rejuvenation, giving you a moment to relax and absorb the day's experiences.

- **Utilize Indoor Attractions:** Incorporate visits to indoor attractions like the Pirates of the Caribbean or the Haunted Mansion into your itinerary. These provide entertainment and offer a chance to sit in a cool environment, which can be particularly refreshing during warmer months.

Moderate Physical Exertion

- **Pace Your Exploration:** Disneyland can be overwhelming with its size and array of attractions. Pace yourself by setting a realistic schedule that includes only the rides and shows that interest you most. Use the Disneyland app to monitor wait times and distances between attractions to minimize unnecessary back-and-forth walking.

- **Footwear and Comfort:** Comfortable footwear is indispensable. Choose well-cushioned, supportive shoes that can handle hours of walking. Additionally, consider lightweight, breathable clothing to keep comfortable throughout the day.

Leverage Quiet Rides for Downtime

Quiet Rides as Rest Opportunities: Rides like the Disneyland Railroad or the Mark Twain Riverboat offer more than just scenic views—they provide a chance to sit back and rest. These rides can be particularly strategic after lunch or during the mid-afternoon slump, serving as a gentle break from the more physically demanding activities.

Mental Relaxation Techniques

- **Mindfulness and Meditation:** Brief mindfulness exercises or meditation can be incredibly refreshing. Find a quiet corner, perhaps near the Tomorrowland gardens, and spend a few minutes in meditation or deep breathing. This mental break can help reset your mood and energy levels.

- **Journaling Moments:** Taking time to jot down experiences in a journal serves as a wonderful keepsake and can be a relaxing activity. Find a café or a quiet spot like the seating area at the Royal Street Veranda and spend a few minutes reflecting and writing. This offers a break and enriches your experience by allowing you to process and appreciate the moments of your voyage.

Embracing Solitude in a Lively Environment

Navigating the energetic pathways of Disneyland, a realm designed for communal joy and shared excitement, can seem daunting for those who draw energy from solitude. Yet, within this seemingly ever-active world, there are ways to embrace quietude and carve out moments of peace that allow for a deeply personal and fulfilling experience.

Selecting the Time of Visit

- **Choosing Off-Peak Hours:** One of the most effective strategies for finding solitude in Disneyland is visiting during less busy times. Early mornings, late evenings, and weekdays during the off-season typically see fewer crowds. During these times, the pace is slower, and one can appreciate the ambiance without the overwhelming presence of large groups. These hours provide shorter ride queues, quieter dining experiences, and less congested walkways.

Utilizing Quiet Zones and Lesser-Known Paths

- **Finding Hidden Retreats:** Disneyland is designed with several quiet areas that many guests overlook. The pathways around Tom Sawyer Island, the alcoves near the Royal Theatre in Fantasyland, or the gardens adjacent to the Tomorrowland Terrace offer tranquil spots. These areas are perfect for taking a break from the sensory overload, allowing visitors to recharge amidst natural beauty and relative quiet.

- **Exploring Alternative Attractions:** While major rides draw large crowds, there are numerous low-key attractions and exhibits throughout the park that offer calm and engaging experiences. The Animation Academy in California Adventure, for instance, provides a cool, dimly-lit environment where one can draw and learn about animation in a peaceful setting. Similarly, the Great Moments with Mr. Lincoln exhibition offers a quiet, introspective experience away from the crowded throngs.

Mindful Planning and Navigation

- **Strategic Itinerary Planning:** Careful planning can significantly enhance the ability to enjoy solitude. Use the Disneyland app to monitor crowd levels and wait times, planning your route to avoid congested areas. Incorporating rest periods into your schedule at strategically chosen times and locations can help maintain a sense of calm throughout the day.

- **Dining Off the Beaten Path:** Choose restaurants and snack spots that are away from the main crowd pullers. Dining during off-peak hours or at less popular venues ensures a quieter meal and enhances the overall enjoyment of your culinary experience without the rush.

Personal Space in Public Settings

- **Managing Personal Space:** Even in crowded settings, you can manage your personal space by using headphones to listen to calming music or ambient sounds. This creates a personal bubble and can help mitigate the impact of the surrounding noise and activity.

- **Enjoying Shows from a Distance:** When watching parades, fireworks, or live shows, consider viewing from less crowded areas. Though these might offer a slightly different perspective, they provide a more relaxed experience, allowing you to enjoy the entertainment without the discomfort of being in a dense crowd.

Engaging with the Environment on Your Terms

- **Photographic Walks:** Engage with the environment through the lens of a camera. This activity focuses your attention and allows you to connect with your surroundings on a deeper level. Photography can be a meditative practice, helping you see the beauty in details that might otherwise be overlooked in the chaos.

- **Journaling Your Experience:** Take moments throughout your visit to jot down your thoughts and observations. This serves as a wonderful keepsake and can be a reflective activity that allows you to process and appreciate your experiences in a more intimate manner.

The Importance of Breaks and Self-Care During Your Visit

Visiting Disneyland, a place brimming with excitement and activity is an adventure that stimulates the senses at every turn. However, for those who prefer quieter environments, the constant stimulation can quickly become overwhelming. Recognizing the importance of breaks and self-care is crucial in ensuring that your Disneyland experience remains enjoyable and does not lead to burnout.

Understanding the Need for Breaks

- **Mental Rejuvenation:** Continuous exposure to large crowds, noise, and visual stimuli can saturate the senses and diminish your ability to enjoy the experience. Regular breaks help reset your mental state, reducing feelings of overwhelm and sensory overload. They provide an opportunity to process and appreciate the experiences of the day, making subsequent activities more enjoyable.

- **Physical Rest:** Disneyland involves extensive walking and standing. Without adequate rest, physical fatigue can set in, making it difficult to navigate the park and enjoy the attractions. Scheduled breaks allow you to rest your feet and refresh your body, which is essential for maintaining energy levels throughout the day.

Strategic Break Planning

- **Finding Quiet Spots:** Disneyland is designed with numerous quieter areas that can serve as perfect spots for taking breaks. The lesser-known paths of the Redwood Creek Challenge Trail in California Adventure, the tranquil seating areas around the Royal Theatre, or the shaded benches near the Disneyland Railroad stations are ideal for relaxation away from the crowds.

- **Timing Your Breaks:** Plan your breaks during peak attraction times, typically midday, when lines are longest and the park is most crowded. This provides a reprieve from the crowds, and it is an efficient use of time. Enjoying a leisurely lunch or sitting down for a coffee during these times can be particularly effective.

Self-Care Strategies

- **Hydration and Nutrition:** Regular hydration and nutritious meals are vital, particularly in the energetic and often sunny environment of Disneyland. Dehydration and hunger can exacerbate feelings of tiredness and irritability. Carrying a water bottle and snacks like nuts or fruit can help keep your energy levels stable throughout the day.

- **Protective Gear:** Always prepare for the weather. Sunscreen, a hat, comfortable footwear, and layers of clothing for varying temperatures are crucial. They protect against environmental factors that could otherwise lead to discomfort and hinder your enjoyment of the park.

- **Mindfulness and Meditation:** Integrating brief mindfulness exercises or meditation into your breaks can significantly enhance your mental well-being. Even just a few minutes of deep breathing or a short meditative pause at a quiet spot can restore a sense of calm and control.

Leveraging Technology for Self-Care

- **Disneyland App for Planning:** Use the Disneyland app to monitor wait times and strategically plan your breaks around your location in the park. The app can help you find nearby quiet areas and alert you to less crowded times for attractions, optimizing your rest periods.

- **Digital Detox:** While staying connected is important, constant connectivity can also lead to stress. There are periods during your visit when you disconnect from digital devices to immerse yourself fully in the experience and engage more deeply with your surroundings.

Embracing the Experience at Your Own Pace

Recognize that each visitor's endurance for crowds and activity differs. Tailoring the pace of your day to match your personal comfort level is crucial. This means not feeling compelled to see and do everything. Prioritize quality over quantity in your activities to ensure that your Disneyland experience is memorable for all the right reasons.

By emphasizing breaks and self-care during your visit, you safeguard your physical and mental health and enhance your overall experience at Disneyland.

Conclusion

As we conclude this guide to navigating Disneyland for those who prefer a trek less trodden, it's essential to reflect on the unique joys that such an experience can bring. Disneyland, often perceived as the quintessence of exuberant family entertainment, also holds a multitude of layers that cater to the quieter, more introspective visitor.

The Joys of Experiencing Disneyland as an Introvert

For the introvert, Disneyland's magic isn't just in its thrilling rides and vibrant parades; it also lies in the subtle details and quiet corners of the park. There is a profound joy in observing the meticulous craftsmanship of each themed area, from the rustic streets of Frontierland to the futuristic pathways of Tomorrowland. These details often go unnoticed by the typical visitor but can offer deep appreciation for those who take the time to look closer.

The early morning hours, when the park gates first open, present a world of possibilities. The air is cooler, the light is softer, and the crowds are thinner. This time allows you to appreciate the sounds of the park waking up—the distant train whistle, the gentle music drifting from the speakers, and the sound of water flowing through the rivers and moats that crisscross the landscape. These moments, though fleeting, can offer a profound sense of connection to a place designed for making magical memories.

Embracing Your Unique Travel Style

Every traveler brings their own set of preferences and needs to their tour, and understanding and embracing your unique travel style is crucial. If large crowds and noisy environments feel overwhelming, planning your visit during off-peak seasons, utilizing FastPasses to avoid long lines, and knowing when to take a break can help manage these challenges. This guide has equipped you with strategies to navigate the park efficiently, ensuring that you can enjoy the attractions at your own pace and retreat to quieter spots whenever necessary.

Remember, it's perfectly acceptable to skip the must-sees if they don't appeal to your interests. Disneyland is a vast park with diverse attractions; what resonates with one visitor might not hold the same charm for another. Tailor your itinerary to include the experiences that you find most fulfilling, whether it's a leisurely stroll around Tom Sawyer Island or a quiet cup of coffee at the Market House on Main Street, U.S.A.

Final Thoughts on Finding Magic

The real magic of Disneyland doesn't just lie in its larger-than-life characters and exhilarating rides; it also exists in the quieter moments that offer a reprieve from the usual bustle. Finding a secluded spot to watch the sunset, enjoying the intricate details of a favorite ride, or discovering a new path are all parts of the Disneyland experience that can be particularly rewarding.

Additionally, integrating moments of mindfulness and reflection into your visit can enhance your appreciation of the park. Whether it's pausing to enjoy the floral arrangements on Main Street, U.S.A., or sitting back to watch as other families create their memories, these moments of quiet observation can provide a unique sense of fulfillment.

In essence, your trip to Disneyland should be a reflection of your personality and interests. With the strategies outlined in this guide, you are well-prepared to explore the park in a way that suits your introverted nature, allowing you to embrace both the excitement and the tranquility that Disneyland has to offer.

So, wear your badge of introversion proudly as you discover that even in a place filled with crowds and noise, there are countless opportunities to find joy, wonder, and maybe a little bit of magic, all on your own terms.

Printed in Great Britain
by Amazon